The Stolen Poems of Sophia Batts

SOPHIA MONIQUE BATTS

Rainbow Shop Hawaii, LLC.
Honolulu

Rainbow Shop Hawaii, LLC.
Ewa Beach, Hawaii
96706

Rainbow Shop Hawaii, LLC. is a publishing enterprise located on the Island of Oahu, Hawaii.

First Edition: December 2018
Published in the United States of America
ISBN: 978-0-578-42372-2
Library of Congress Control Number: 2020922714

Book Design by Sophia M. Batts
Cover and Pictures by Sophia M. Batts

This book is dedicated to my inner child,

Little Sophi

Foreword

Sophia was 36 years of age, dealing with Bipolar and Diabetes Type 1. She had a husband, two children and a wonderful life in Hawaii. Suddenly, things took a drastic turn for the worse.

Initially, this book stemmed from a place of anger, frustration, depression and mania. Sophia nearly lost her life on the streets of Oahu, Hawaii. After losing most of her material possessions, she lost her freedom for sixty days in the throes of a Manic Bipolar Episode. Subsequently, in writing this book of poems, she has gained humility, confidence, faith in God and a newly found outlook on life. Hopefully, some motivation can be drawn from the words that pour from her heart. Sophia has grown stronger and capable of overcoming any obstacle. By not ever giving up on herself and watering her faith, she is now able to conquer every endeavor she faces. Others can draw inspiration from these poems, living their best life with peace, happiness, love and laughter.

Ronnie Lee Batts

Author's Note

I was born in 1981, the Year of the Rooster. 2017 was yet another Rooster Year on the Chinese Zodiac Calendar. I cocked my way right through it, seeing a light at the end of a dreary tunnel. Getting my life in order and waking up to a new reality, I have persevered through significant struggle. Only I know who I am deep down inside and what I am capable of. My book of poetry is meant to inspire and motivate others who have suffered or are suffering; I strive to put a smile upon the faces of the downtrodden. I now know myself better because of this manuscript. This collection of original poetry was written in 60 days while locked up in a Community Correctional Center in Oahu, Hawaii. Cockfighting & clawing my way back to sanity & reality after a year's long journey, I truly believe I am The Rooster standing Tall and Strong.

The Rooster: As Explained by a Xerox Chinese Zodiac 2017 Calendar

"Rooster people are very observant. Perhaps you can say that Roosters have a very keen "sixth-sense." Roosters always appear attractive and beautifully turned out. Their minds are very perceptive, making Roosters excellent trouble shooters, detectives, doctors, nurses, and psychiatrists. You rarely see a relaxed rooster that sits quietly, doing nothing. They are also multi-talented and can become accomplished in many different ways. Though sharp, practical, and resourceful, the Rooster also likes to DREAM. Roosters make great hosts and adore Entertaining. The main virtue of the Rooster is loyalty; they make devoted friends. They always keep their promises and are always true to their word. When Roosters love and admire someone, they will go to great lengths just to keep them happy!"

CHAPTER 1

My Youth

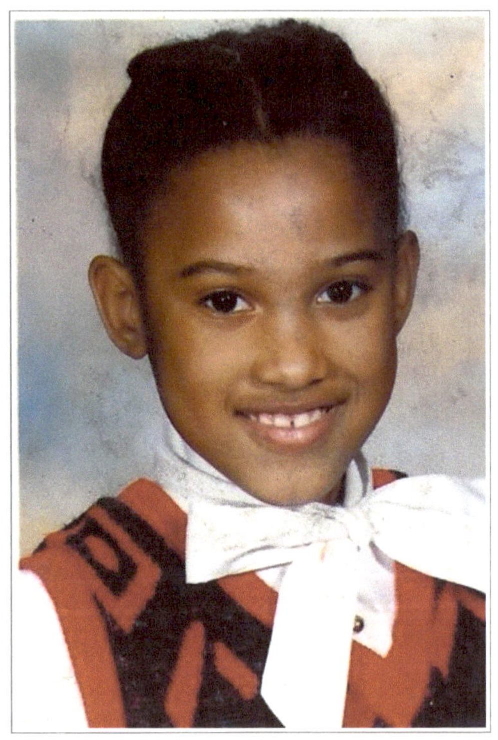

Bubblicious

Life is like a bubble…

Extremely Fragile.

It is fueled by an iridescent array of color:

Red, Orange, Yellow, Green, Blue, Indigo, Violet.

Upon death...

The bubble is relieved of its transparent husk.

Bursting forth...

Only fragmented traces of its immortal existence.

Caged

How did I become a caged animal?
I must ponder the idea.
Just yesterday,
I was frolicking freely with the pride, swimming with dolphins and becoming a dove.

Now I'm trapped!
I can't run, can't hide, can't look up!!!
I guess I'll just slide aside, back down into the ground like some old earthworm,
Burying my colorful spirit when it would rather Soar, Dancing!
There's still time…
A Single Hope,
One Wish….
One day I Will Fly...
Far, Far Away…

Before~

I'm caught again!
Like a Caged Bird,
I Will Not Sing.....
Those melodious tunes which when combined provide Harmony.
I'm scared!
Life is like a traffic jam, and I'm stuck!
Until I have the Right of Way,
I'll Stay…
Content!

Down To You

Angel Divine,
Rendered Sublime…
With an awe-inspiring charm you enchant me.
Bathed in a celestial black light,
You dream through night,
Unscathed by the dusty dawn or ethereal sun burning bright.
A Noble Knight and Gallant Prince,
You charge into battle armed solely with Reverence...
And Enlightenment Profound....
A Knowledge Unbound….
The simple sound of a soothing tone is worth more to me than all the gold
I could possibly own.
You…
Shake the Walls of my Internal Sanctum.
Subsequently, the Exterior Melts.
To feel what I have felt, I Must Be Blessed.
For if not progress of self....
Then there is nothing left…
But..
You.

CHAPTER 2

Comedy

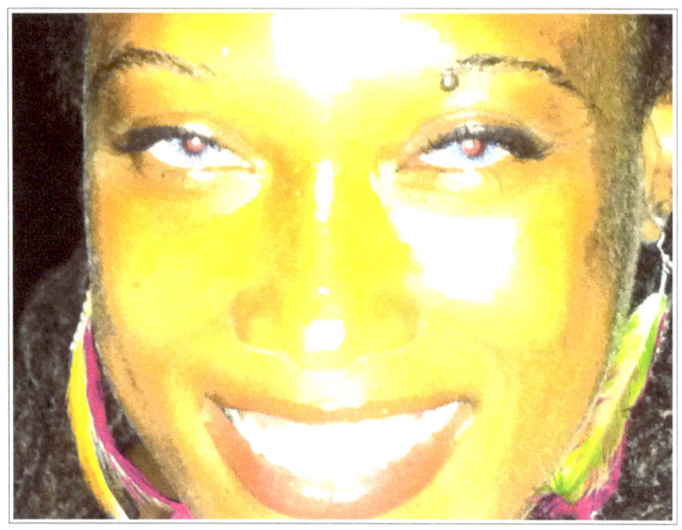

"I'm Rich Bitch!"

Like Dave Chapelle say, "I'm Rich Bitch!"
...In every single way.
No matter what & how much you take away from me,
I will get richer everyday.
Check out Richie Rich from Da Comics…
I am carefree…
Like he, I get paper!
I ain't neva no broke bitch!
I am forever rich!

An African once told me,
"In Africa, ANY Trace of Blond or Gold Hair on a Black Body makes you Rich!"
Even if I have not a dollar in my pocket,
With Golden Hair upon me,
I am Rich for Eternity!
Even if I have not a dime, nor a pot to piss in,
Staying broke and poor;
I will never be broken & destitute actually,
Because,
Secretly,
I have golden hairs all over my body...
Meaning, I'm one rich ass African!

"I'm rich bitch!"
Run tell dat Insignificant and Jealous Hoe,
"Don't you dare snitch!"
You rat faced, witch of a broke ass, hustler type wanna be…
Hating, Thieving, Undercover Bitch!
'Cause you know and I know…..
SoSo run dis shit!
She can Definitely spit!
She own Da Ritz…..
Po' Pimpin'
Rockin' and Clockin' Deez Hits!

Haters Gonna Hate!

Hate On you Fuckin' Haters!
Each day, some asshole will attempt to deter you with their HATE!
Let that ignorant muthafucka go on and hate.
Laugh it up stupid fucker, right in my face.
I can taste the fowl negativity on the tip of your tongue.
Unfortunately,
For You,
Snitch, Witch, Bitch,
It is I who win & won.
I am the only one.
It is only you who sin….
To covet what and who I am or own…..
My Life,
Personality, Character, Integrity, Morality, Style, Class, Manners,
Ass
Super Bella,
Power,
I Tower Tall!
Let me shower your dumb, hating ass with my luv!
The Almighty Father Above might forgive you for acting like trash…
If you let that hatred dissolve so we can solve our dispute,
Letting the tempest storm pass.
Be brave, Be stealth…
Not insecure & unconfident over my incredibly gifted, fine, talented self.
Get yo' life together, taking back your own abilities & capabilities,
Building Amazing Wealth.
I know in my purpose given to me by GOD
Himself,
I am going to win…
Rising Far Beyond Hateful Sin and Petty Bullshit.
I shall undo my own sparks of fury,
Holding Back strife caused by anger,
Keeping negativity at bay.

I will use God's example of keeping my pride in check with good self-control.....
Being slow to anger that way.

While haters continue to hate,
I'm gonna Ball like Mike Jordan
'Cause Ballers gonna Ball....
Bulls #23 style Dunkin'...
You can't see me.
You haters gonna Fall,
Wanna be OG!
This Chiraq-y, Sassy Girl
Is a Black Pearl...
A verbal gymnastics killa who is way illa than you.
You'z ain't nothin' to me...
But a fuckin' squirrel looking for a nut.
Kiss my Butt,
Grimey Hater!

BooBs

Boobs,
Beautiful Boobies….
They come in all shapes and sizes.
A woman can be an A cup, C, Double D, H, B or even G.
It is okay to have pink versus black colored areola with a couple of strands or two...
Surrounding the exterior of a female's passion hue.
Who told you the truth about titties and tatas?
You'z just disgruntled because you got stuck with Bad Genes & Bad Luck,
Given less than other ladies in your sight,
Producing two baby mosquito bites on a flat chest which is Not Right!
Boobs get ENGORGED
So us women can feed a village of keiki three square meals with snacks everyday.
The keiki are the babies who yearn & crave for sweet, mother's milk.
Mother's milk is nectar...
Like honey flavored manna from heaven...
A Gift!
Those infants are especially lucky to get that good drank that makes their Brains Grow…
Healthy, Intelligent & Strong.
Helping them Think Better…..
Can't go wrong with breast milk for babies.
However,
Some women like Bosoms & Boobies simply for Style.
Slice 'em, Dice 'em, Add a water bag or two,
And make 'em stick out
Plump!
Lookin' like Janet Jackson who played with the Nutty Professor in that movie with The Klumps.
It's True!
Breast Augmentation is a New Gift,
A Fabulous Fad for the Nation.
"It's a Celebration!"
Like Rick James used to say.

Everybody Loves a Juicy Titty,
Unless you belong to the itty-bitty titty committee.

Let us Embrace them...
Before they catch cancer and Fall Off!
Or you can hack them off,
Surgically Removing your Best Asset
Through Mastectomy.....
Like the actress, Angelina Jolie,
Doing Preventative Maintenance
On her Big Boobies.

CHAPTER 3

Epiphany

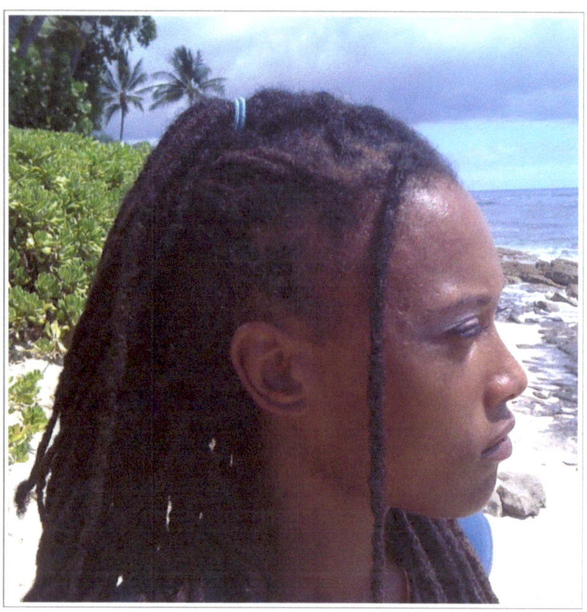

Patience

Patience is a virtue and something to strive for.
Everything will Happen,
Coming to Fruition
In Due Time.
There is a Time for Everything...
So stay Humbly Patient!
Do Not Be Bothered or Burdened…
By Waiting in Line…
For your turn to come…
Now!
Be not Hampered by Patiently Waiting.
The Reward will be Much Greater,
If...
You can have unwavering Patience!
Your maker will be Proud,
Blessing You Beyond Measure.

Brevity

If my life were to end tonight,
I would have lived the most wonderful life
I could have possibly dreamed.

In my life,
I've already died a million times....
From heartbreak and tragedy.
Misfortune...
Sweet Luck!

I don't give a fuck anymore!
No longer in a rut,
I'm free...
Impossibly free!

I live to savor each day.
The simple brief moments
Enjoyed Tenderly.
Fleeting memories...
Of hope.

All is not lost.
Cherish what you've got...
Before you have not.

Live It Up!

Live it up…
Bad Boy, Bad Girl,
My Boo, My Gym Shoe!
Go Berserk, Go Crazy, Go Cock-a-Doodle Fuckin' Doo!!!
Be Who U Wanna B, Flying High…
Do what You Have to Do,
And KEEP Doin' yo' Thang!
ALWAYS Try and Strive.
My Jigga Type Nigga, Swaggin' it Out!
My Precious Queen, So Stunning, Divine and Fine…..
An Elegant Lady,
You Rockin' it out Right!
We shall accomplish ALL Our Dreams, living it up Supremely Tight!!!
In this life, you only got One to Live…..
So Live it up to the Fullest Kid,
Creating your Own Biz.
Take it All the Way UP to tha Tippy Top!
Neva Eva stop for them Doubting Haters….
You and Me, Baby, shall Ascend to Heaven,
Triumphantly Overcoming Every
Trial & Tribulation,
Gloriously Gobbling up Goals….
We will WIN!
Astonishingly Toppling Over & Defeating…
Wondrous Plans we Plot…
If we Fall Down,,,
We Will Get Back Up
Again!

Nappy Like I Like It!

In the New Millennium,
Curly Hair is in Style and All the Rage!
Hotter than Hot, Phatter than Phat…
Tight Curls are Back!

Nappyness Reigns Supreme!
Natural hair on colored girls is currently Rocking Out the Glamour Scene!
These young, forward thinking ladies Rock Rough and Tough
With their Afros, Curls & Puffs.
They are Super Bad and shall Rock their Locs Forevermore.
These brazen young girls, as well as older women, are confident and independent,
Not caring any longer if you call them
Nappy-Headed, kinky or bushy haired,
Unrelaxed, uptight or bald head slave…
Even Buck Wheat, Sideshow Bob, and Kunta Kinte type names Cannot Phase them
Bold,
In Control,
Intelligent, Well-Educated, Sophisticated,
Hard-working, and Positively Progressive Women.

In this day and age, ladies have wised up,
Gaining a new found thrill,
Letting those gorgeous, elegant locs blow back in the wind,
Being able to keep it real & chill.

To live with natural hair: curly, coarse, thick & knotted…
Is a proud gift.
Take 100 strands of curly hair,
Knot them up & bind them together…
The hair will grow long, longer and Longer,
Never Stopping,
Hardly Breaking,
Just holding Firm and Strong.

That's what I do with my Locs of Love!
My dreads are ready when I awaken and roll out of my bed.
These Kinky, Healthy, Long & Strong Locs of Love are Super Knotty, Twisted and Nappy Like I Like It!
Girls, don't be fooled by some smooth, straight hair talking, boozer type nonsense.
Both our hair and cultures are rich, thick and complicated.
Just love & adore the curly, fine, divine locs that you handle with skill.
Do them thick locs up fresh to death, whippin' them buttas 'til they absolutely ill…
Rockin' them curls, dreads or braids that are
Oh So Sick...
So Totally Legit!
Be Forever Proud of the God Given, Natural Locs you were born with.
Your Curly, Good Hair is Immaculate!

Sun Shine On Me

Sunshine, sunshine…
Washing me.
Sunshine, sunshine…
Bathe over me.
Sunshine, sunshine…
Soak into me.
Sunshine, sunshine…
Make me feel free.
Sunshine, sunshine…
Free to be Me!

Vampire Soul Sucker

The way you latch on to me is totally devastating,
Steady biting into my neck, mind, body and soul.
Using my pounds of flesh to prolong your own life is Not Right!
My lifelong sacrifice is akin to the worth of Pure Solid Gold.
I can no longer give my blood all to you….
I am growing weary, weak and So Very Old!
It is time for me to be wise,
As well as a bit selfish,
Taking back my spiritual essence...
Paying myself with True Unconditional Love Bold.
Please just Let Me Go!
You are steady sucking me dry…
I am beginning to turn COLD!
You are destroying me outside & in…..
You Vampire Soul Sucker!
You are a Sin.
I will never let you drain me dry, kill me and win!
I am the unbreakable, unstoppable, undefeatable, unshakeable….
KIN…
Of GOD!

Flying Free

I Never Ever want to be a Beggar or Haggardly Hag…
Roaming the Cruel Streets carrying a Bulging Trash Bag!
Please believe me,
God is the Only One who can Judge Me.
I plan on becoming all that I can possibly be...
In This Lifetime….
Conquering God's Purpose for Me,
Given to me by He…
To accomplish in order to reach self-actualization and self-realization,
Attaining my wildest dreams.
Before Death Becomes Me,
I wish to Fly Free!
Like the True Leo I am, My Lion will, one day, Run Freely with the Pride!
I will remain gentle and humble within my spirit inside,
As I Rise,
Ascending to Great Heights...
Another Level or Plane of Existence….
In a Whole New World or Dimension.
I'll reach the Highest Heights...
Like a White Owl in the Night,
Soaring,
Hunting Prey,
Taking Flight.

Triple Rainbows of Hawaii

GOD made mankind a PROMISE…..
After the Great Flood of Noah's Time,
All over the earth's floor.....
The Everlasting Torrential Tempest Downpour….
There would be a Pure & True Rainbow to signal the end of it all.
A time of peaceful tranquility after the winds blow and raindrops fall.
Some people have only witnessed one or two rainbows at a time,
Sublimely resting colorfully behind the silver lining of clouds
In the midst of the sun in a rainy sky.
If you are lucky like me, you could see Three!
A Triple Rainbow!!!
But only in Paradise
On a Tropical Island Chain known as HAWAII.

No Smoking

I got a Lighter...
In Shaky Hands, Ready Too....
STRIKE a Cigarette!

CHAPTER 4

Sophistication

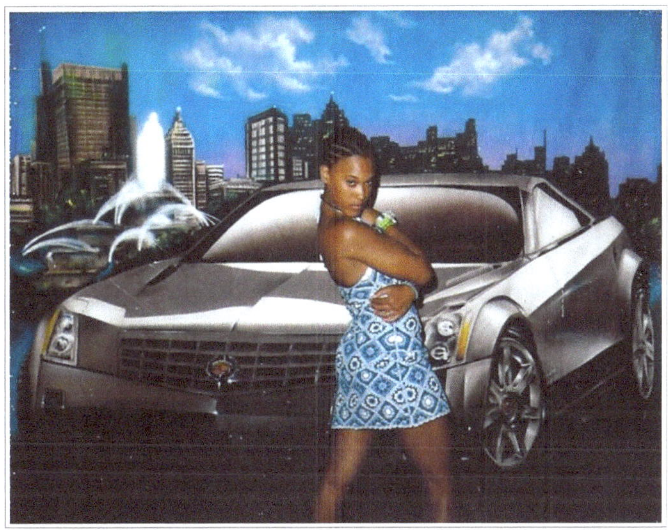

Attack of the Pretty People

Beautiful, Pretty People have Life the Worst!

Every mean, dark thing or human being thirsts for their inner niceness and or outward Beauty.

Evil People Lust after the Pretties, hurting them by inflicting Pain, Harm, Torment and TORTURE, Flawing them like it is their Duty!

Thus, pretty people become flawed & insecure, Remaining Afraid.

Unable to fight back from Lames playing Trickery Games on their Minds, these kind, good-looking people become undone, losing sight of the Perfection into which they were Made.

Unkind words & actions create Sparks of Fury in Pretty People who become Filled with Strife, Rage & Clouds of Anger ready to Explode or Burst!

It is hard to Cope!

When there are Meanies all up in your gorgeous face, telling you that No One likes you or that you are Absolutely Nothing, you must acknowledge your own greatness, letting Love for Yourself internally within your heart Sing!!!

Put Your Pretty Self First!

The Creator made you Phenomenally Perfect as you are, Awesomely Amazingly Something, so Let Joy Ring!!!

Although Negative people and Negativity will attack a Pretty Person leaving them Feeling Cursed, they are far from their lowest point, their Absolute Worst!

Know, you are a Pretty Person, and you are Not Alone or Possessed, for there will Always be Haters that you must Love due to all their support and respect, however Never get Too Sad or Too Lonely taking your Pretty Beauty away from this place called Earth by committing suicide, Ending Up in a Hurst!

Love Me in a Special Way

Love me in a Special Way,
Because I'm a specially made woman, and I deserve respect, kindness, gentleness,
Genuine Sincerity, sensitivity, security, protection, Shelter From Any Storm...
Plus,
Compassion, truth, tenderness, Comfort, righteousness, Faith,
Sympathy & Empathy, Motivational & Inspirational Support,
Interest in my ingenious ideas & intelligent creativity,
Belief in my spirituality, and Queenly Worship Toward Me.
There should be...
Absolutely.....
No bullying or being ungentlemanly, controlling me & manipulating.
I need no negativity or demands!
Because...
I am an Angelic Spirit, and I want to remain slow to anger and grounded
Like God's example teaches me,
With an optimistic outlook,
Sub-doing any spark of fury,
To avoid exploding into rage and creating strife in my life....
Keeping my demeanor and facial features Ever so Pretty,
Cute and Nice!
You want to know me?
Stay hopeful, support me fully, uplift & progress my mind, spirit and my soul...
We can grow old together,
Forever Positive,
Achieving Massive Success,
Making Magic and Miracles Happen,
Completing our Life's Purpose given to us by God,
Making and Earning our way into Heaven....
With
True, Passionate, Undying
Love & Respect!

A Real Lovely Lady

A Real Woman is a Queen:
High-class, Eloquent, Elegant, Supreme!
She is like a Fine, Exquisite Pearl
In this World filled with Empty Oysters.
A True Lady knows how to utilize her Power & Sexuality to her Advantage,
Enhancing her Tender & Gentle Prowess
By turning up the charm to Maximum Strength!
Pheromones wafting through the air mixed with Ambrosial Perfume:
Floral, Fruity and Sweet...
Strategically Sprayed on her Voluptuous Body in Misty Plumes of Fragrance.

Using her Smile, Finesse & Femininity,
Plus her Strengths,
She fully understands how to Excite, Entice and Prey on a Man's Weaknesses...
Like a Lioness Stalking and Hunting her Prey,
Be it an African Monkey out in the Jungle
Or a Gazelle Running Free out on the Serengeti.

The Real Woman has got it Going On!
Never Too Easy or Easily Swayed,
She can have it Her way.
The woman can work Her Mind & Her Sexy Va-jay-jay;
She is Independent, Strong, Fiery, Unafraid, Confident with the Pu-Nani....
And Above All,
Lovely...
Like a Genuine Lady!

Orgasm

An orgasm is like an EXPLOSION within one's loins.
During the experience, there is a gradual build up filled with hot, smoldering passion,
Intense aching, and a tickling tingle that ignites a Fierce Burning Desire....
A Deep Longing, making Sexual Promise & Sexual Hunger Swell.
The hunger that swells inside the woman is Wet & Throbbing.
I cannot say what happens to the man.
All I know is that the clitorus is the lustrous button you press and play with that sparks
Lascivious Dreams, desire, and lust.
My cream pie is silky like satin.
When the button is licked or pressed...
The deliberately quickening force sends deliciously multitudinous thrills
And thigh shaking, rippling chills within & throughout my body,
Producing an electrifying jolt I cannot ignore.
That sensational feeling makes me thirst for more.
I become provocatively brazen while vigorously and invigoratingly rising Higher, with
Sexuality Seething, climbing up, Up, UP in Absolute Ecstasy
To a greater, more amorous plateau.
The sensations of arousal one can feel are incredible!
A Burst of Sexual Hunger sweeps over the Soul!
The passionate heat is so Fierce and Fiery, making you BOLD!
You may even have to bust out the Secret Diary,
Jotting down,
The furious, lovely sex you have found.
Don't be reluctant!
Just Go For It!
Nakedness is nothing to be Embarrassed about.
Tremendous roaring lust awaits.
You can even Masterbate...
Moderately...
Making Multiple Orgasms...
Over your true love who has you under their spell...
Or bust a Side-Splitting,
Pee-Pee Squirting,

Creamy and Wet,
Projectile-Shooting Orgasm
All over the place…
And their beautifully gorgeous face.
Only about 40% of women experience an orgasm in bed.
Maybe, the other 60% simply need some mind-blowing head.

CHAPTER 5

Family

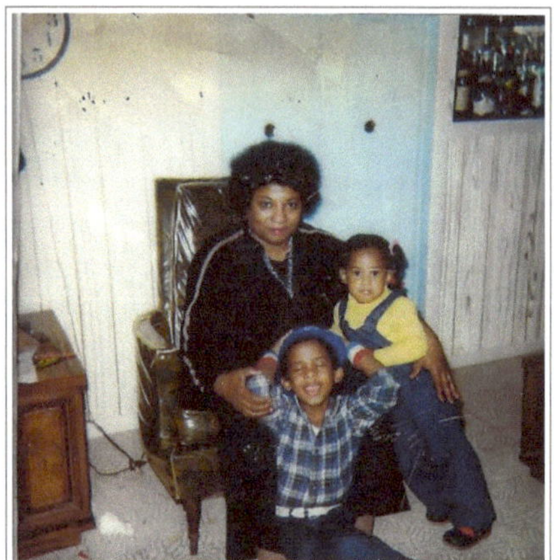

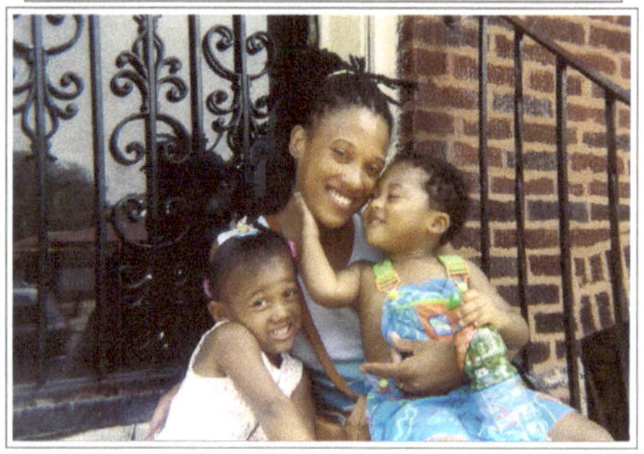

Rainbow...
Color Me Home

Rainbow...
Can you color me?
Rainbow,
Please, set me free.
Rainbow, can you please color me HOME???
The Rainbow Maker, he shall Release Me, rescuing my spirit & soul by
Coloring me away back to my original home…
Where I came from.

Sun Rays melt into me….
Moonlight Beam Melodies….
Drizzles of rain come shower me,
Washing over me, cooling my body down.

The rainbow hidden beneath the dark clouds high up there in the air,
Will color me home, I do not fear.
I now know,
I am never alone or on my own,
When rainbows
Hidden colorfully in cloudy skies
Come to carry me
Through Trials,
Back to my loving family at the home
In Chicago
Where I once belonged.

Fine As Blackberry Wine; My Mommy Told Me

My Mommy, Rosemary, Told Me;
Baby….
You'z like a Sophisticated and Complex
Fine Blackberry Wine…
That gets Better, Finer and Sweeter as it
Matures & Ripens over time.
So Sublime & Divine...
The Ambrosial Scent…
With a Delicious,
Exceptionally Flavorful & Juicy,
Succulently Sweet Taste…
So Miraculously Heaven-Sent!

Hawaiian Sophi

My name is Sophia Monique Prater.
Secretly, I am insane in my bipolar brain.
My family knows I have a mental illness.
They put me on pills called Geodon,
Keeping me Sedated & 'Down to Earth,'
Because they believe I'm psychotic & deranged.

However, that is not me really.
I am a uniquely special snowflake with an original,
One-of-a-Kind Pattern.
I was raised, traumatized, on the slave-like Prater Plantation,
Whipped and beaten with switches at the bottom of Pill Hill...
Where the black doctors lived so fine.
I aspire to beat diabetes by being My Own Doctor.
I have an amazingly beautiful mind.
So I Shine,
Brighter and more illustrious than other people.
I'll never be normal,
So they don't understand me.
I talk & think faster,
Look better without makeup,
Think & Dream,
Somewhat
Bigger than the rest,
So they cannot get wit' or see we.
I am also sort of slow & stupid.
Hustlers always put me to the test,
Steady robbing me...
Leaving me baffled over how they were able to gaffle my shit.

Though I have very little street-smarts,
I have incredibly phenomenal book-smarts in my pocket.
These tools can help me to rule my own fantastic world;

I am skilled giftedly in dance, meditation, swim, floetry, creative writing, art, poetry,
Painting, photography, Fine woodworking, cabinetry, teaching, collage-making, and
Communication...
I speak Ebonics fluently...
Plus,
I can handle the English Language with Proper Pronunciation;
I am able to Enunciate Every Word with no Hesitation.
My name means Wisdom,
Thus I Am a Beautiful Black Pearl,
Blazing Positively in the Light of a Brilliantly Bright World.

When I was just a small, skinny, cute, little Girl,
People would remark,
"You are the Hagia Sophia...
The last remaining Cathedral in Spain,
Dedicated to the Goddess Sophia who was exiled from Heaven;
You are The One!"
Later, I learned Hagia means Holy,
And the Hagia Sophia is located in Istanbul, Turkey.
So, am I like the Holy Sophia?
Were these people all being real with me, or were they just poking fun?
Alex Grey has exquisite art representing her spirit,
And there is poetry featuring this elusive goddess, Sophia;
She's The Real One.
The Quaternity is what they called her heavenly family
Before Sophia made her fall from grace.
She was like me, a Moni....
MORE unique than all the troglodytes, and Maybe, she liked to Prattle On & On &
On TOO MUCH; unbeknownst to me, Prater does mean Foolish Talker, you see.
Is that why she was exiled from heaven so negatively?
'Cause she ran her opinionated mouth too much?
Maybe God got annoyed and fed up, with a Tremendous Headache,
Over all her Mental Gymnastics and Thunderous, Fast-Paced Sounds,
Uncontrollable Noise like the Clattering of Symbols.

Sophia gave birth to three: hope, faith and charity.

She may even be Christ's Mommy.
Since the dawn of time, EVERYONE mistook her for the Holy Spirit!
Let's try not to get too religious, talking about some shit I don't really understand.
Just know,
I am a child of God, and I can do anything I put my mind to,
Because that Supernatural, Heavenly & Almighty Man
Don't make no junk!
I ain't never no punk.
Call me Hawaiian Sophi.....
Soon and very soon,
I will rule again!
I'm that Mango Redbone Weirdo you can't stand to see...
So you steady dialing up police on me!
I married a Batts, and I had three of his babies...
Kai & Rom live on.
Reemus is gone.

Kai-Rom is the greatest, most precious creation I ever made & know.
I helped them grow, 'cause I ain't slow.
I'm a Fast Ass Little Girl, as constantly stated by my Auntie Grace Renfroe.
I flow tight, I rhyme right, I reach higher heights that others cannot ascend to and go.
Like my Mommy do, you may just want to call me So or SoSo.
I'm no Professional PhD. OB/GYN Doctor like I planned
Or Genius Rap Artist like Dr. Dre; he's the skilled, music-making Pro.
I'm just trying to get my life together so I can make it, in my dreams, on Death Row...
The Label, that is!
However, I ain't tryin' to get Electrocuted and Fry or Die like 2Pac & Biggie
'Cause I'm So Fuckin' FLY, and I SOAR High up in the Majestic Sky.
I wanna be the Phoenix, ascending from dust & ashes,
Flying straight back
To the Illusive Galaxy hidden Deep in Orion's Belt....
Like in "Men in Black."
I Rock Out!
I'm a Smooth Criminal who is brave, strong, & stealth.
Like Secret Squirrel, this resourceful black pearl of wisdom shall figure it all out.
I ain't ever gonna be no Dead Trout, Floatin', Stankin' on the Ocean Blue

Or on Lake Michigan at 95th Street Rainbow Beach.
Or found dead in a garbage can like my other Granny, Carrie.

I was born Cook County Free...
Grew up on 93rd Cregier near South Side Stony…
In Chicago a.k.a. Chi-Town, The Windy City,
Also Chiraq; a term coined by Spike Muthafuckin' Lee.
When the Hawk come down, you'll Definitely See Me…
The Prettiest Angelic Baby...
Batt-Woman....
Motorcycle Flying in my Blue Sketcher Thick Soles on LSD (Lake Shore Drive).
I was raised on the South Side of the Chi on Stony Island.
Now, I'm rocking it out on a Rocky Island, & I LAVA YOU!
We so freakin' cool livin' in Paradise on Oahu…..
The state capital of Hawaii is right here in Honolulu!
My birthstone be Peridot from the tears of Pele.
Her tears are stuck, dotted & wedged inside & out of Lava Rock....
Found only in Hawaii.

And like Hawaii,
My nickname and middle nickname both have an I that sounds like a long E.
That is why I call myself
Hawaiian Sophi a.k.a. Moni…
The Super Fantastically Fabulous, Radiant & Eloquent, Talented & Gifted, Spiritual, Soul-Searching, Angelic Goddess, Phenomenally Amazing, Trail Blazing, Leo Lioness Constellation situated shining in outer space, only Totally visible from afar…
The Absolute Dopest Super Nova Star.
I have no doubts or qualms, we shall Go FAR!
I am Technologically Savvy like the Millennials.
Plus, I drive a Smooth & Luxurious Mercedes-Benz, E-Class, Car.

My Daddy Drove a Stankin' Lincoln

Over 30 years ago,
Way Back in the Day,
My Birth Father, Da-Da, used to pick me up from Amelia Earhart Elementary…
He would say,
"You wanna ride on my lap?"
I'd say, like the late Gary Coleman,
"What you talkin' about…..Willis?"
He would take me for a Ride...
Sitting me on his lap, Gripping the steering wheel
Pretending I could Drive
His Stankin' Lincoln.

The car was Tan as could be.
The back seat was comfy for me,
But it Squeaked,
Smelling of alcohol from empty beer bottles and cans sprawled out on the floor
Beneath my dangling feet.
My favorite excursion on the way to the After-School Program at the 111th Street YMCA, was our couple of stops to fill up on gas, candy, cookies and beverages at the Gas Station or Bubbles Liquor Store on 93rd & Stony.
My absolute favorite, passionately loved drink was the Mr. Pure Papaya which had a Punch of Sweet Flavor.
I would savor…..
Every last Sip & Drop!

After dropping me off to delight in after-school fun & play,
Plus my many classes at the 111th Street Men's YMCA,
Austin Junior would Leave Me…..
Driving off in his Tan Stankin' Lincoln.....
Into the vast beyond!
Sometimes, I might get a little sad, with a depressed frown.
Yet, I could always turn that frown Upside Down…
Into a SMILE...

When I saw my Papa pull into the driveway, one hand on the steering wheel,
High Spirited, Jovial & Alive with his own Happy Smile ready to greet me!

He would bring home four or more movies from Blockbuster Video:
Faces of Death, Rosewood, Remo Williams and The Miseducation of Little Tree!
I wholeheartedly believe my Da-Da Absolutely Adored Me,
Even though He Didn't Raise Me…
He tried to be the Best, Most Caring Father…
The Daddy he was able, willing & could possibly
Be.

Cruisin' in the Caddy on Vogues

I used to be Cruisin' in the Caddy on Vogues with Grama and Grandad,
Loving the Eldo…
Rado, that is.
I was just a little kid,
But I can still remember floating down the freeway in a Luxurious Eldorado Cadillac
With a lavishly laid, leather interior,
The outside Black as the Night Rider!
Grandad was paid, so he could Floss!
That car,
My favorite vehicle,
Sitting on Vogue Tires,
Would float like a butterfly:
So Smooth, So Sleek, So Cool!
Grandad always drove it right...
Not Too Fast in the day or night…..
At 25 miles per hour, he kept the Eldorado lookin' and rockin' tight…
Midnight black, shining, glistening....
A Gorgeous & Glorious Sight!
You know Grandad bought another Caddy to continue driving down south from
Chicago to Yazoo City, Mississippi once the Eldorado wasn't ridin' right!
The Sedan DeVille was blue and pure white
With Grama and Grandad floatin' it
Down the highway back to Yazoo, again and again, for their family & class reunions...
Taking FLIGHT on I-65.
Living life with the Grands exposed me to what a Cadillac truly is…
An Exquisite Work of Luxury Art
Sitting on Vogue Wheels.
Pristine & Mean...
If you know what that is!

A Rap for Dorris Oddessa

She is FOREVER Radiant & Eloquent in every way…
Elegant EVERY Day!
Extravagantly, she lived her life to the Fullest!
Her Hard-working, Strong, Unstoppable and Determined Spirit…
Paved the Way!
A Master of Quan she was.
Also a well-educated Horticulturist,
She would Always Just Know the name of Any plant or flower.
A Zoologist as well, she Miraculously brought dying flowers back to life,
Resurrecting them with her concoction of Peat Moss, Miracle-Gro and H2O.
My Grand Mother had a green thumb, a knack and a talent for restoring plant life.
Dorris began as a sharecropper down in Yazoo City, Mississippi.
After making the Great Migration to Chicago, Illinois for better jobs and a better life,
She became a house cleaner to Rich White Folks in Hyde Park.
Grandmother was a Gorgeous Top Model at some point...
Silky Fine Hair down her back.
With a degree, she then began to Acquire her Dough as a School Teacher,
Making her Stacks of Money.
Then, with no hesitation or fear, she raised her three sons...
As she became a Business Woman Entrepreneur!
She purchased, ran and controlled a Real Estate Monopoly.
In the End, she owned Ten...
A professional collection of houses, timeshare villas and condos...
Property for her family to be exact...
For Sure...
Dorris Oddessa worked it out well for over 50 Long Years.
Her assortment of Plants, Flowers, Trees & Shrubbery
Made our house the most beautifully colorful on Cregier.
The alluring landscape included a Magnolia Tree out in front
Which I thought was an eye-catching jewel.
Over 40 years of her life was spent teaching at Sullivan High School.
There, Dorris taught Horticulture, Biology and Zoology to the High School Keiki…
The Teenage Adolescent Kids.

Tragically, Alzheimer's Disease set in, slowly eroding her memory.
Eventually, the horrible disease took all her facilities.....
And her heart forgot how to beat, her brain how to think, her lungs how to breathe!
In the end,
She was still,
Lovely.
I know I will see her again...
In heaven,
Because although Gemini,
She was only a little mean,
But Mostly,
She was phenomenally incredible,
Super Sweet, Stunning and NICE.....
Raising me, her only daughter, from age 50 to 85:
Loving, Intelligent, Kind, Generous, Determined, Well-Rounded, Gifted, Talented and POISED to Live My Life.
The Grandest Mother I ever knew, she raised me up...
Doing it just RIGHT!
With her fine clothes, thousands of shoes, 10 real fur coats,
Gold jewelry & Diamonds dripping,
My Superb, Spectacular Granny stole the show,
Keeping it Exquisitely TIGHT!
Her Life was a Testament to the Success and Triumph of One Woman,
Powerful in the Black Struggle.....
The Ongoing Fight....
For Equality...
For Morality, Integrity & Uprightness!
I Will Always Love You...
Dorris Oddessa.
Princess to Queen Supreme...
Be with your Husband in Heaven.
Forever let him, hold you in his arms.
Grandad waited 18 years to see you, pamper you and protect you from harm.
You Grands are my Father and Mother True.
Do watch over me & mine for all time!
Until we meet again,

Go with God!
Be Forever Happy.....
Breathing in Pink & Purple Sky while Exhaling Blue!
GOD loves you!
As I Eternally DO!

Da-Da's Song

My daddy was born at the end of October, close to Halloween.
A real true Scorpio Zodiac,
He sometimes scared the shit out of me, 'cause that man had a Powerful STING!
He Lived the Life Of Riley, because his mother Always took great care of him.
She felt guilty and ashamed of raising all her sons as a Strict, Abusive,
Firm & Aggressive Authoritarian.
Dorris did something incredibly mean to her 3 boys which helped to foster Bad Seeds...
Within each of them.
My daddy never grew up, 'cause he was broken and torn.
He was constantly beaten by his mother,
This creating a Great Tempest Storm
Of Furious Anger in his heart.

At age 12,
He started stealing liquor from Grandad's Bar.
It made him feel good,
Forgetting about his Mama's High Expectations and Strict Discipline.
He eventually became an Alcoholic.
Subsequently, he evolved into a crack cocaine type drug addict due to this trauma.
My dad was still a cool cat.
He always watched great movies from Blockbuster with me.
It was him who taught me to cook spaghetti and his favorite, special chili!
Austin Prater Jr. meant so much to me.

Once I turned 5,
Every New Year's Eve,
He'd let my big brother and I drink all the alcohol we wanted to consume.
He trained us to fire and shoot his Big Guns into a Huge Pine Tree in his backyard.
Being so small at age five,
The Shotgun with the BuckShot would kick me back....
Gratefully, I made DaDa proud...
Always standing solid, hitting my target and handling the kickback well.

My DaDa's favorite beer was Slitz!
He knew how to guzzle it, handling his shit.
He went to the Army.
They sent him to Boot Camp in Hawaii.
Then, he came home to Chicago to work in a Mortuary…
Embalming dead bodies.
He never finished Mortuary School,
Yet he had enough skillz to become a Mortician's Apprentice.

At age 5, I visited my first funeral parlor.
Mommy and Scooter were too scared to even get out of the car.
They both refused to step foot inside.
DaDa always thought I would become an OB/GYN doctor,
So I should have no fear of dead bodies that had died.
That night,
I saw a dead man in a coffin and a naked, bald-headed lady with her tits exposed.
She was a Pasty White caucasian, Pale to the Bone.
All alone on a metal table she lay.
To this day, I can still see her image and her face.

My father was so proud of me when I made valedictorian in preschool and elementary.
Though he drank heavily and beat on my mother constantly, he was exceedingly elated
That I wanted to become a doctor like my cousin, one of his best friend's, Reneé...
Ushering new life into this world
Delivering high risk babies.
He would be the one to prepare bodies for death,
Sending them out of this world into the next.
He thought I should care for him in his old age, buying him a house, a Rolls-Royce,
The luxuries of his Dreams!

At 16,
He beat on me bad, and I rebelled...
Holding a strong hatred deep down inside of my heart for him.
I still loved my daddy,
Going to his family barbecues.
Conversely, I also hated him for beating up Mommy

So Often...
For his Pissed Off Attitude...
For not raising us...
Handing his responsibilities of child-rearing off to Granny and Grandad.
'Til this day, I can't understand him beating the white light out of me
At his house down the street.

My daddy died from 7 strokes on April Fools Day, 2014.
Initially, it seemed like some kind of sick joke to me.
Then I realized, I loved my daddy immensely.
His memory is now one I hold deep within my heart,
So Earnestly....
Eternally.
I surely miss you Pops!
You pimp, a True OG....
Who shows a thirteen-year-old into "Mac & Me" style movies,
"The Mac," to teach her about the birds and the bees!
Only you, Crazy Man!
I hope you are in heaven with God and your parents.
Dear friend and birth father...
Thank you for mending our relationship.
I'm ecstatic you gave me such a wonder-filled life.
You are once, twice, three times a fellow...
A true gentle man.
And,
I Love You
I Really Do
Love You
Dada.

Grand Dad:
The Grandest Father
I have ever known!

Life is a struggle.
Everything you told me was true.
I don't know beans from apple butter.
I learned that from you.
I was only knee-high to a damn duck;
You stood 6 feet like a giant towering over me.
I can still remember looking up at you,
Marveling over my Granddaddy at age 3.
You had the integrity of saints, yet you would never front.
What I loved best is that you were always blunt.

Never drunk,
You worked Chicago Streets & Sanitation as a City Driver,
Never late or missing a day once in over 40 years.
I held onto you tight, crying tears as you carried me, Sophia Monique, Your Niquey,
Up to the podium to accept your Distinguished Award.
It was a Reward representing well deserved Honor!
You introduced me, and all I could see was a sea of faces smiling back at me.
There was a round of applause for your acceptance speech.
Our whole entire family acknowledged your efforts.

You and Granny never really had to take us in,
Because Grandmother was 50, and you all had already raised your three sons,
Satan's Kin.
I guess you and she were sad that these first generation big city dwellers let Chicago get
The Better of them, becoming Drunkards, Alcoholics, & Drug Addicted Scoundrels...
Stealing alcohol from the household bar and your double-door closet.
What in the hell were those 12 year old boys thinking???
Drinking hard liquor from Grandad's bottles...

Then replacing the emptiness left over with water…
Like a bunch of sneaks!!!

I know you knew,
Based on their haggard like behavior and tipsy demeanor.
You possibly cried and pulled your hair out,
Grinding your teeth,
At your wits end over what to do!
I apologize sincerely, Grandfather, for my own shortcomings too…
For not listening to you when you tried to explain reality.
Straying slightly, veering off the path,
Then coming back after a life changing turn around,
Only to sink back down, backsliding...
Now picking my face and body up off the ground.....
I almost died too many times with a haunting frown upon my beautiful face.

I cried deeply for you and, now, Granny
Who passed away this year.
My heart hurts knowing you have both transcended this world,
Although I feel you near.
After 18 long years of separation following your death in 1999,
I know that exquisite & marvelous woman will be resting happily by your side,
Shining right next to your star, forever loving you:
Her magnificent husband,
Her dapper, cool cat,
Her boo!

Dear Grandad,
You are a good, great and gracious man…
A King who did Everything for us all...
His and your cherished family…
GOD has been watching over us from above.
Fear not my Grandest Father;
We will make it despite any major setback, obstacle, or hurdle in our way.
This is a new day.

Grandfather, beloved Grandad, the year is 2017.
That is 18 years that you have been dead and gone away from me.
I miss you dearly, because I can no longer call you weekly...
Hear your voice respond as I give you all the updates over the phone...
I am utterly alone in this cruel, unforgiving world so dark and lonely...
Only my family stars are my friends.
I can count you all on one hand, just like you said!
Just as You taught me!
I miss you So, and I love you, I love you, I love you...
You must know.....
For I only had 17 years to grow under your tutelage.
During that time, brighter and more vibrant I shined!

It is only due to your love that I continue to rise above pettiness to higher heights
Taking flight like a Phoenix bird...
You created a dove out of pure, unconditional love…
That is why I adore you so!

You were just crossing the street (running your plumbing business from pay phones,
'Cause you didn't believe in cell phones) when that vehicle hit another car, lost control,
Jumped the curb in your direction, sweeping you right off your feet.....
Smashing and throwing your tall body up over 20 feet into the air!
You dropped and fell down so hard on the pavement, body broken and bloody.
It was not fair for God to let this happen to such a Good Man like you.....
Letting the devil try to kill you,
Breaking and Smashing your strong limbs into.....
¡Smithereens!
Like only some demented devil would do.
Later, you explained to me how you actually died twice.....
Then came back to life screaming, "Sophia!!!!"

You refused death at those Critical & Crucial Moments in time,
Knowing that you Couldn't & Wouldn't Leave Poor Niquey Behind!
It is OK Grandad…
You lived to see my face.....
Hug, Hold, and Embrace me again.

I'm Heartbroken you got well after Two Long Years,
Just to get sick from cancer,
Having to deal with More agonizing pain...
Only to Die all over again.
I will love you forever & ever....
In case you did not remember or know!
You gave me all the tools I needed
To Learn, Succeed & Grow.

I will try to stay strong…
I will try not to mourn….
For your soul may be reincarnated in my son first born!

Mi Familia, Dead & Gone

I used to run from life's problems.
Now I face them head on.
I used to feel small & defeated.
Now I stand Tall and Strong!
My family warned me to Stop Running Away and Come Back Home!
I did not Listen,
Now they are mostly dead & gone.

Grandmother Died: 1-15-17...
She raised me as my Soul Mother, teaching me all I needed to know to be all I could
Possibly, potentially be.
My father passed away: 4-1-14, in his sleep.
Dreaming, he drifted away peacefully.
Grandfather Died: 10-31-99, on Halloween!

I will always cherish my Grandfather, the Grandest Father I have Ever Known.
Now here I am standing in a Hawaiian Paradise…
Older and All Alone.
Only the stars above watch over me, some of my Last True Friends.
I plan to succeed at all my endeavors....
Live a life worthy of honor,
Then pass away at age 85 like Granny, Dorris Oddessa Prater.
I will make my way into a Heaven of Splendor & Grandeur
Unlike I have Ever Been Shown,
Ever Before!

It is up to me; I am the Baby.
Most of the Praters have departed from this world.
Time for me to be a Splendid, Radiant & Eloquent Lady.
I must Rock It Out on my own,
'Cause I am utterly alone.
Missing my family of origin so incredibly, heartily and fearfully,
I know I will make it farther than anyone hoped for little Sophi...

For I am a Shooting, Super Nova Star.
I will go far beyond this cosmos, straight into a New Dimension, Out of this World....
Into another happier, more positive galaxy....
Becoming all I am meant & destined to be.....
Despite horrific trials & tribulation, much unnecessary suffering.....
I shall forevermore be totally free!
Transcending this life and this world we live in.....
Ascending to the Heavens in a Heavenly Chariot for my Sad, Sorry Soul who is worth
Much More than Misery, Diamonds or Gold.
I am getting old, weary and weak.
Time to Lay it Down, cry into my pillow, and I will eventually fall back to sleep...
Back to my dreary, dreamy wonderland where I escape every night for 2 to 4 hours,
Hoping to see my Prater kin and family again!

Never Fear,
Sophi a.k.a. Niquey is always here for you...
You each & You All have a genuinely beloved place in my Black wHole of a Heart.
Know,
I will Love You Forever!
We shall Never Part,
Mi Familia,
Absolutely Never!
With your spirit living within me,
I can Conquer Every Endeavor....
I Face.

CHAPTER 6

Love

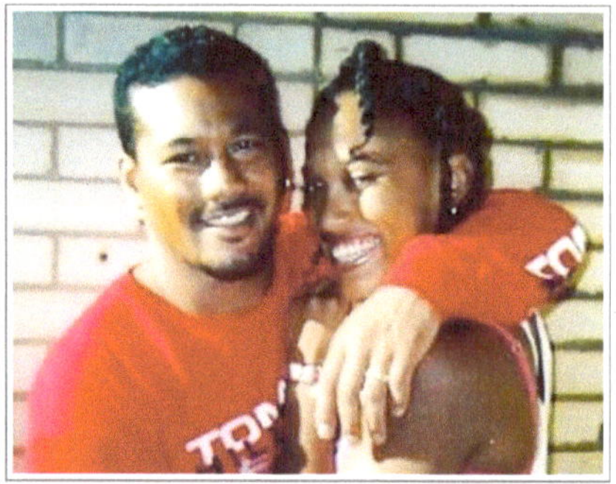

Reemus Aurius-Rio Orion-Lion Batts
Due: 8/9/17 ~ Died: 3/13/17

My sweet baby boy is an angel divine.
It is so sublime that God was kind enough to give you life within me....
Even if just for a moment in time.
This she-wolf was not as strong as I should be.
I lost 25 pounds of flesh.
Then, I lost you on 3-13-17, my son, at only 18 weeks.
You were perfectly formed,
A miniature human being...
Curled up into a fetal position...
Your eyes open to see.
You looked up at me
Staring wide-eyed in my direction.
With light pink skin so glossy, smooth and wet,
I imagined you to be supremely supple,
Yet I was too traumatized to touch you,
Feeling your angelic, perfect self.
I cried deeply as the Chaplain came, and the nurses whisked you off.
They did bring you back,
However.....
You were swaddled up in a blanket, warm and delicately soft.
We said a beautiful, heavenly prayer, sending your spirit & soul up to God
To be with your ancestors old & dear.
I believe and know, without a doubt,
Grama, Grandad & DaDa will watch over you in heaven.
GOD, will keep you safe from Misery, Suffering and Despair.
I shall never fear, as I hold you near and dear to my heart.
Our Spirits & Souls are intertwined, and we shall never be apart.
Reemus Lee, my infant lion cub, you are The Rooster like Mommy,
Sent to earth swimming all around, so fast, in my belly.
You are my Little Lion King.
You will Always reign Supreme...

Angelic Being.
On the constellation Orion in space above…
I see you soar…
My super hunter-warrior, 3-Studded Nova Star.
You shall be forever made Leo...
A Kingly Lion in your second constellation of stars.
I will watch you bravely hunt in the night sky from planet earth afar.
Until we meet again, my handsome gentle baby...
My Lifelong Friend.
This is not the end!
In the Year of the Rooster, 2029...
When I am 47 years of age,
Hopefully
We,
Your daddy and me,
Shall try to conceive you at the end
Of October
All Over Again.
I pray we win!
If not,
I will never stop loving you,
My second son;
Your blood and spirit I now carry within….
Keeping us connected.

Miloski

Milo, Dear Milo, I miss you so…
My baby bro, you mean the world to me.
Smart as can be,
You are everything I wished you to be
Which sets me totally free.
Service dog extraordinaire, no one or anything can compare…
To the unshakeable bond we share.
A true show dog,
You strut your Silky, Soft Stuff.
You Prancercise,
Wagging that tail....
Soft, Hot, Furball, Critter Fluff.
They call you Milo, but you were born Hawaiian so it's Mēlo.
The I makes a long E sound like the I in the name of paradise, Hawaii!
I like to say,
"MeatLoaf, No Onions Please!"
Little MeatLoaf a.k.a. Milo (Mēlo) is a Maltese/Terrier mixed breed with a Mohawk.
In over 10 names, they call him: Toto, Benji, Cujo, Scruffy Doo sounds so insane.
I like Beauty and Beast because DRU HILL's Beauty is his name.
Women go wild for his beauty and the fact that he is so tame.
When I remove his leash and he runs faster than lightning, I call him, "BULLET!"
Like Foster the People, "all the little kids with the pumped up kicks" can Never Run Faster than My Bullet.
Milo MeatLoaf is also known as Boo-Boo, Hanna-Barbera Style,
From Yogi the Bear…
He is Simba, my lion king who is a very special service animal I hold close & dear.
He is a diabetic alert dog, my D.A.D....
Trained to sniff, smell and detect high or low blood sugar within me.
He does not bark or bite, yet he will bully you with his love.
Milo can kill and annihilate you with his licks, kisses & hugs.
Milo (Mēlo) means shade tree in Hawaiian….
Thus, Milo hunts and protects me throughout the night.
Then, he always chills in any shaded area during the day.

Chillin' like a villain, Milo hides out shaded under car, bench, tree or chair.
Little Milo doesn't really care if he is a dirty boy.
After his cleansing bath, Milo rolls around on the ground, on top of grass, without a Single Care.
Nothing is cuter or more adorable than his dirty face; my baby cries real tears.
His favorite food is salmon with the skin and rice.
This, plus his Caesar diet of Filet Mignon does his blond and white, silky coat Good and Nice.
Milo even sips on milk like a cat would.
Sometimes he acts all persnickety, not wanting to eat his Puppy Chow
Like I know he should.
This puppy was made for the Big Screen.....
Already potty trained when I rescued him from the Humane Society
At 11 months old.
I was incredibly lucky that he was not sold.
Amazingly, he was born on the same day as my daughter: Milo 2015, Kaiya 2001.
Milo is only one year old.
I adore him from the depths of my soul.
My Baby Boo Love, Milo, means absolutely everything to me....
He is such a Good Boy...
All that I hoped, wished, and DREAMED that a doggie would be!!!
Now....
It is time for our Runway Show!
Here come the Dynamic, Tag Team Duo...
Sophi & Milo!
Together...
They are One Spectacular Show Dog Show.
They call the dog Miloski tha Broski
a.k.a.
Milo, my little bro.

Pico

Pico's Da Guy Yo!
Anywhere I go, he will go.
A rescue dog, he is a little skittish.
Learning very slowly, he is quite a bit timid.
Pico pees & poops outside after eating the puppy chow from his doggie dish....
My one true wish.

He is like a little fox with a red coat, apple head and white chest.
At about six pounds, this long-haired chihuahua boy will not rest.
Until I lay down,
Not making a sound.

With so much energy,
Pico only wants to play.
He is so cute, friendly & happy!
The baby boy knows where his home is, and he loves me everyday in every way.

I cherish my tiny toy dog so much,
A Blessing sent by God above.
I Saved his Life from Euthanization!
Now, he follows me with no reservations.

He is such a good boy;
We will always love each other
For Life!
We will grow up.....
Together Forever,
Despite...
Living through challenging difficulties occurring in both our lives.
We will strive to be the best we can be...
So that we can survive.

Kaden

Kaiya Sonique is my Favorite Little Girl in the Whole Wide World.
She is Sweet as Apple Pie and
My oh My…
She is Supercalifragilistic-Expialidociously Bright!
Oh so Fly!
Oh so Unique!
Behind those big wide curious eyes and the demure beauty which appears outside,
Lives a Remarkably Talented Wiz Kid....
Forever Genuinely Sincere
With famous artist skillz by age Eleven.
She draws her inner self as Asian...
In purple paint glitter...
Crying yellow star tears that float up to heaven.

Though her appearance looks Peaceful & Calm on the outside,
She could be laughing her Ass off at you,
Busting a Gut inside
Her Smooth Demeanor.
Kaiya is Flyer than me, her Mommy!
Totally as Cool, Flamboyant & Radical as can be!
She call me Cra-Cra….
We have fun & play...
Doing exciting adventures everyday, ecstatically in the sun…
She is Perfection…
A living, walking, growing, changing, talking version of me...
My Reflection.
She is Number One.
My First Born
Precious
Baby Love.

Debonair Rom

It is so Astonishing to me how I could be the Mother of Romulus Lee....
This young teen Pisces Prince Lion Cub is the One!
He swims Upstream as a Pisces, hunting prey like my Lion Cub Baby!
Savant-like & Strong, he will Never Be No Punk Pussy,
Never Ever No Scrub of a Man!
Raised by a Lovingly Fierce Ram Type Sheep...
A Lamb dressed in She-Wolf's clothing,
Romulus will live on!
My Precious Handsome:
So Special, So Humble, Totally Charming, So Cool, So Pensive, So Amazing,
So Resilient, So Tough!
He is my Favorite Teenage Boy in the Whole Wide World...
My Dynamic Illustrious Pearl...
A Diamond in the Rough.
He is Phenomenal and Definitely Tough Stuff!
A force to be reckoned with.....
I can't Ever diss him,
I gotta Hug & Kiss him,
'Cause he is my Sweet, Sweet....
Much Sweeter than Pudding Pie or
Peach Cobbler Pie.
You'll Love Him
Wit' his Fly, Extraordinary Personality.
Quiet & Calm, he'll make you Laugh Uncontrollably...
And Cry...
With his Sophisticated Wit, creating Jubilant Laughter, Tickling you Pink.....
Romulus has become a Real Man,
Extremely Gentlemanly and Very Dapper.
He is Debonair!
I Really Do Care and don't want him caught up by some Gold-Diggin', STD-infected
Slut Witches!
They'd Better
BACK THE FUCK UP!

Muthafuckers...
Them hatin' ass enemies of my Son…
You gonna get it!!!
Homie,
Hawaiian Sophi Don't Play when it comes to her Handsome Cub...
Her Baby!
No worries Son,
I got your back from Infinity into the Beyond.
Rommie, Rom,
My Romulus…
An Engineer Scientist at Heart,
He will be Rich Internally,
Someday, Someway,
'Cause the Name is Romulus Lee…
He's Rom Lee, Bitch!
Get it Straight....
Get it Right....
The Man is Bright and Outta Sight!
You Feelin' Me???
Do You Feel Me?

All of Me, Given to You

I have loved you for a lifetime.
Ever since I met you,
I've been devoted, giving you my all.
Every fiber of my being...
My mind, heart, body and soul.
I am your loving doll.
When I'm together with you, I light up inside.
So honest, I have nothing to hide...
I swallow my pride…
Let's keep it Real, your Divine Self is Mine!
The light of your face shines Incomparably...
Beautiful and Sublime.
You Are My Strength….
Let's Stay Together for All Time!
Securely, I rest in you….
You've had my mind and heart from the start.
Love, true love, resounds.
My heart still pounds.
I have found that you help me to clothe myself with Kindness, Compassion,
Patience, Humility and Gentleness.
There is absolutely no distress...
When I give my all to you...
My gorgeously beautiful baby boo!
I always knew we would and should be together forever,
Me, giving my all to You!
Never leaving you...
Never will I forsake you!
Absolutely All of my spirit, soul and being Belong To You!
United, we shall never falter & fall!
Baby Boy, you know for sure
You got my All!

Vows

With this ring I to thee wed...
Two hearts beating together spiritually connected as one...
Two souls intertwined until the very end of time!!
Loving you in marriage,
I give you All My Love.
My mind, heart and body sincerely Adores my King;
You mean the Entire World to me, making my heart Sing!
Cherish me and we shall remain Together Forever, Forever Together In Love...
Heavenly, I believe you were sent to me from God Above!
I shall be Faithful and True....
Let us begin again, Bonded Forever, Anew.
Please love me in a special way boo!
All this love I have stored up inside my blue heart, I will shower upon you.
Instead of alone and on my own, I will stay with you.
Stay with me until the end of time if you so choose.
Never dishonor me...
The Queen Supreme, Spiritual Angelic Being;
I have seen enough pain, hurt and suffering to last a lifetime.
I need your gentle care, positive support, inspiration, motivation and genuine sincerity
To bring me inner peace, harmony, trust unwavering and absolute serenity!
You are My Man.
I will forever love you!
Throughout this lifetime, our love will endure.
I will still love thee
Beyond an infinity of time...
For an Eternity!
You are now Mine.

Don't Give Up!

Everyone needs words of empowerment & encouragement…
So they may never get weary & weak while attempting to accomplish a goal...
Therefore...
Giving Up!
Let us do as Mother Hen reaping her wheat bread harvest.
We shall practice hard work in the face of obstacles and turn a cheek to doubters,
haters and naysayers who oppose us, trying to block & deter us,
Standing in our way...
Attempting to undermine us while hobbling our bones.
We can & will accomplish our dreams all on our own...
Needing no one or nobody to help us but ourselves and our own minds!
You know deep down, we got this work finished & done
By the grace of God!
Then, in due season,
We shall reap what is owed…..
A Heavenly Harvest, worth the weight of Solid Gold!
If we Faint Not...
Keeping Hope, Faith, Dedication,
Plus
Hard Work with Patience & Perseverance,
Determination & Well Doing in our Hearts.
"Don't Give UP" is the Good & True Motto for Today!
If we remain Resilient,
Marching forth like a Stallion...
Steady Reaping,
At the proper time,
We shall gather a Plethora,
A Heavy Heaping...
Even More than One Can Imagine!
But Only….
If We Do Not Give UP!
We shall SOAR, Gaining So Much More....
Than you know or thought possible.

God is Great, Glorious, Almighty & Awesome!
He makes us Capable of Seemingly Impossible Feats.

Jigga

What up Jigga,
a.k.a.
My Nigga?!
You are my Luminous, Shining Star
That Glitters, Sparkles and Gleams from afar.
I Miss You Dearly!
I wish I could find you.
If I did, I would leap into your body!
Picturing your Sexiness & Charm,
I cannot stop smiling!
A gentle touch...
Your warm embrace...
Some shit that's too hard to explain.
You've got the mind of a King...
Lookin' Hella Tight...
Just Right up in them Jeans.
They are extremely becoming on you,
Mr. SUPA Dupa Sexy...
My Boo!
I know if I was on you & your
Awesomely Handsome Body,
I would be coming too!
You so Hot and Fabulously Fine,
I wanna make you mine!
I could eat you up wit' a plate of sausage biscuits and some gravy,
Baby!
You got me goin' crazy...
Homie Lover Friend.
Because,
I want them Passionate, Mesmerizing Eyes
On & All Over Me
Once Again!

Fruitful Beginnings

How could I love you knowing…
That generations have set us apart.
One look into your eyes, and I melt upon your warmly genuine heart.
It is your body, being and soul I wish to explore.
It is no wonder that your ship crashed into my shore.

I am like a Sweet, Succulent, Savory and Adorable Peach...
The Absolute Sweetest Peach…
To be exact.

You are like a Tangy, Tart and Well-Ripened Pineapple…
Deliciously & Dynamically Sweet...
With a Delectable, Delightful, and Exotic Taste,
Breaking my mouth with an Amazing SMACK!

Together, I have no doubt we would make a Pretty Phenomenal Pear.

CHAPTER 7

Sweet Treats

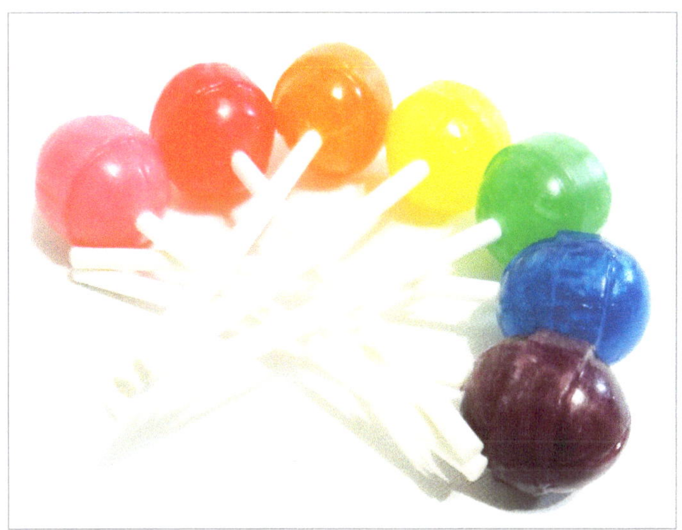

Ode to Ice Cream

I adore my creamy ice cream.
Each flavor is tantalizing to the tastebuds & tongue…
So Icy Cold and Sweet….
Each and Every Ingredient,
UNIQUE!

Please let it be…..
Rocky Road, Chunky Monkey, Pralines & Cream…
Breyers, Ben & Jerry's, Baskin Robbins…
Heavenly manna-like nectar of GOD...
Churned Cream Supreme!

Let it be an Original like Häagen-Dazs Butter Pecan,
My Grandfather's Favorite...
Including World's Finest Chocolate Almonds
Atop Old-fashioned, Homemade Vanilla...
A Combination So Grand it Rules the Land!
Grandmother's Favorite was Rainbow Sorbet she called, "Sherbert,"
In a Plastic Gallon Container,
Yet what I was diggin' on was that Neapolitan Tub Flavor!

Oh yes, I Love Ice Cream....
Though it freezes my mouth, mind, teeth & brain.
The pain of a brain freeze releases tension within me;
I go insane with a head EXPLOSION I cannot control or tame.

The Sugar Rush I get from a 3 Scoop, Ben & Jerry's Waffle Cone
Puts me at a higher frequency level...
An even greater plateau….
Let's do the Waffle Bowl!
Flavors so incredible and totally cool, so worth every penny,
All my Dough!
They even have meltingly delicious soft cookies…

Gimme some thick Chocolate Chip Cookie Dough!

I want some of that Strawberry Cheesecake Graham Cracker Swirl.....
More Birthday Cake,
More Chocolate Fudge Brownie & PB Doughble Fudge!
Those Tasty Jimmy Fallon & Stephen Colbert Flavors...
That sweet stuff leaves me begging for MORE!
So ONO are The Tonight Dough & Americone Dream...
My mouth & face be Broke Off on the Floor!

Ice Cream,
Sweet Ice Cream.....
Please, may I have some More?!

Jamba Samba

Jamba Juice.....
Jamba, Jamba,
I Samba Inside.
Because you have Every Especially Healthy Fruit Flavor under the sun,
Hidden, blended powerfully within each size: small, Medium, or LARGE.
You give me chills.
The myriad of flavors is so incredibly ill.
I can even create my own Fabulous Flavor....
Then take a Chill Pill...
Sitting still, as my heart races....
Chicken skin...
Gooseflesh all over my body created....
Then a Brain Freeze, Ooo...Wee!!!
Do it to me Jamba!
Their juicy fruit smoothies are extraordinary,
Making me feel Sensationally Free!
I will sip you Fast,
I will sip you Slowly.....
Taking advantage of Every Ounce of your Healing, Rejuvenating, Passionate Nectar.
You Resurrect Me.....
Mind, Body, Heart & Soul.....
With your ever so tasty Fruitilicious Goodness: so mouth-watering, so creamy, so sweet.
The Jamba Samba I dance within the depths of my heart can never be taken away
From Me....
For it is my Heart Song, My Spirit Release...
So Break Da Mouth & Break Da Face
Dreamy!
The sense of stress I daily endure is Instantly Alleviated...
Emotional Passion, Inspiration as well as Motivation Awakened...
Each time I Delve Inside...
A Styrofoam Large Cup of Jamba Juice...
With that Tiny, Little Cup of Extra, Leftover Blender Drippings on the side.
Sipping from that itty-bitty cup & tiny, orange designer straw,

I do an Internal, Happy Jamba Samba Dance in my mind every time.
The Blessedly Blended Barrage of Creative & Juicy Flavor makes me Cry.....
Tears of Joy!
Then, I can pass out & Die...
Of Harmonious Happiness.

Ode to OCCC Commissary!

Commissary,
Oh sweet wonderful O Triple C Commissary.
The feeling of anticipation and hunger is so great,
I cannot wait to eat a Buddy Bar and Twinkie Cakes.
Global Brands Old Fashioned Assorted Lemonade Hard Candies take the cake with
Pink, Peach, Raspberry and Regular Lemonade.
I'm in jail without bail money for a $3000 bail release,
But I get Commissary,
Because my Hubby put $40 then $60 on my books for me!
We will see, very soon,
Exactly what my stash of Goody Treats and Hygiene Products will actually be.

I plan to receive everything I ordered, yet one cannot be picky…..
It is always a surprise, never no guarantee!
I smieyez while jumping up-and-down inside…
Because I don't want no hard up, criminal type putas breaking into my
Metal Foot-Locker Box,
Robbing Me!

They want the hot stuff I got, plus anything they can stuff in their bras or draws like
Snickers Bars, Maui Onion Big Bags of Potato Chips, Doritos Cool Ranch, Good
News Bars, a Fantastic Pay Day with Nutter Butter Cookies, Lil' Old Dutch Maid
Chocolate Chip Cookies, Strawberry Pop-Tarts,
Plus da Ritz Crackers with plain M&M's and Mixed Nuts to top that...
Setting it completely Off the Chain!!!

I'm not talking no more smack.
Everyone needs commissary,
Especially Me!
It tastes so good cuddled up in my bunk during lockdown...
The world in my mind's inner eye lights up Brilliant and Vividly.

Now, it's time to shop store.

I pray and hope I get everything I ordered.
If not, I will pop a THOT for taking my spot, and sucking up all the Goodie Good Goods...
The Shiznittles I had wished to see.
Baby, baby....
I got a body that's Bangin' like yo' Banyan Tree...
So Pretty, Hot and Temptin' as can be.
Now Feed Me.....
Snacks, Treats, Cakes & Cookies, as well as Candy.

Mahu Cookies: OCCC Style, Oh So Sweet!

I'm locked down in jail at O Triple C!
I am now in desperate need of some Mahu Cookies…
They are totally Triple D:
Delicious, Delectable, Delightful!
These Sweet Decadent Desserts
Cannot be Beat!
They are the Absolute Best Jailhouse Treat.
Please, please, Please…..
I beg of you O Triple C…
Gimme some Mo'....
'Cause them Mahu put they foot off in dem Cookies.
Fuck One, I could eat about 3 or 4.
Shortbread, Oatmeal, Peanut Butter…
Big, Hearty, Scrumptious & Divine….
Super Meltingly Soft or the Crispy Hard Kind.
I aspire to make all these Amazing Edibles Mine!
Like Dora Say,
"So Delicioso!"
Gimme some more!
I wanna explore,
How to create them myself when I am released from jail on $3,000 bail.
This Smooth Criminal shall Quickly Inhale
A Bucket of these Fantastic Fantasies with their Intensely Enticing Aroma.
Then I plan to faint, passing out from Ketoacidosis…
In a Diabetic Coma!
No worries Bro'….
These delicacies are so Ono…
I'll definitely Live to Eat Me Some Mo'....
By taking 20 units of Insulin through my insulin pump,
'Cause I ain't no punk,
And I am not dumb!

They got that OCCC recipe online for me!
Good Ol' Jailhouse Cookies,
Here I Come!

CHAPTER 8

Fantasy

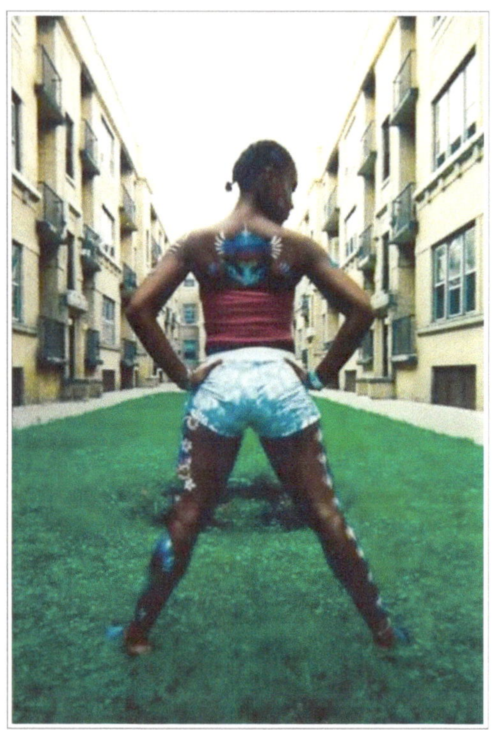

I Am Rainbow B*Right (Bright): So Golden, So Sophisticated, So Tight, 'Cause My Mommy Made Me Mulatto

Rainbow must B*Right in Mind, Body, Spirit & Soul.
Her heart must beat steady, exemplifying the worth and purity of 24 karat gold.
While dynamically remaining and sustaining the weight of a single dove-like feather…
She must be bold!

Her bubbly, sparkling light must endure ignited.....
Continuing to shine psychedelically, serenading us with passionate positivity...
Blazing Beautiful...
Never Ugly...
While reverently serving peacefully & humbly childlike,
The Omnipotent Lord God Almighty.
Using his example of love & being slow to anger,
I shall subdue the sparks of fury that enrage me...
Alleviating anger that is ever so dangerous for me...
By Savoring the Sweet Joy, the Goodness of Life.

By Maintaining an Optimistic Outlook on Life,
I will Defeat Gloominess & Strife with a Happy, Creatively Colorful Spirit,
Shining Amazingly Brilliant in the air surrounding Perilous Pits of Despair...
Letting my Locs of Love Blow Back Brilliantly in the Hawaiian Winds...
With a Kaleidoscopic Collection of Colors:
Pink, Purple, Blue, Turquoise, Brown & Gold.
Blowing back through Trade Winds & Vog,
My colorful locs shall penetrate the Smog.

I will hit those meanies with a rainbow & kindness...
The Utmost Respect!
One can learn a bunch from any person...
I Bet!
Like what to Do and what Not to Do….
How to Act!

Life is Learning: a University, a Teacher.
Reach Out, and Help your Fellow Brothers & Sisters,
Because we are all Struggling to Survive...
Stay Alive...
Working to Make Money to Live our Lives…
Not feeling so Deprived of Life's Good Happiness & Joy….
Not to feel so much Pain & Hurt Deep Down Inside the Gut & Mind.

It is up to me…
Rainbow B*Right to Shine my Eternal Light.
Helping as many souls as possible by inspiring & motivating them to attain their True Life's Goal & Personal Dreams.
The more people I help, the richer I will be.
However, my riches are not monetary.
They are internal.
The simplistic sound of a pleasantly spoken tone...
Is worth more to me than all the dollars & gold I could ever possibly own!

Now,
I'm in the Zone.
You are never alone….
Rainbow has got your back!
I will Attack The Evil One who is hurting and destroying us,
Annihilating him with my Storm-like, X-generation Powers,
Sweeping him away with Tempest Storms & Hurricane Winds,
So he will Never Hurt Thee or Me
Ever Again….
With his Temptations: Hellfire, Anger, Fury, Rage, Strife, Struggle and Sin.
The Devil is a Lie!
God is Good all the Time!
Let's SMACK Satan right in the chops so that we can win.

I Be Rainbow Bright,
Raised Up on 93rd & Cregier….
From that Chi-Town, Windy City, South Side Stony Island, Pill Hill Neighborhood!

Shining ALL of my Fantastically Good….
Smart, Kind, Special, Amazing, Blazing, Fiery, Fierce, Ferocious, Furious, Feline Leo
Lion Type Style of Lightning, Brilliantly Bright, Intensely Hot & Heated, Molten Lava
Fire Light that I acquire from my element the sun.
I will burn that demented devil Up,
Blasting his Evil Ass Away!!!

As a Soldier Strong, a Tough Warrior for God,
My Mommy, Rosemary, made me a mulatto rainbow mixed with
Black, Caucasian and Cherokee.
Bravo, Rose, for creating me!
Now, it is time to Kill the Devil that is Hurting Us All...
By the will of my heavenly father, my phenomenal GOD who watches over us...
Helping us to Not Ever fall from grace.

Believe in him and you Will Not Fail…
God will save Thee like he Blessed and Rescued Me…
We will not Fry or Burn in Hell!
We will instead Fly Up Higher Than High,
Soaring like Eagles,
Creating Ribbons of Colorful Rainbows
All across the Sky…

Once we die, having accomplished God's Given Purpose for Each of Us,
We shall ascend back home to Heaven,
Just like Jesus and each one of us...
Meek, childlike and humble, in that number…..
We shall see GOD.

This is the words of a Mulatto Rainbow,
Colorfully Mixed Up,
'Cause Rosemary is Really a Fair-Skinned, Freckle-Faced,
Yellow Bone Mulatto Herself.

Then,
Mulatto Mixed Up,

Her genes she gave me, along with my Daddy's.
Can you Believe,
Rosemary, My Mommy, Made Me Mulatto?

A Little Mixed Up,
I am the Toughest Soldier....
A Strong, Invincible, Unbreakable, Undeniable
Warrior for God!

Starlight, Starbright

I can visualize my Spirit Animal,
My Unicorn Souljah Rastafari....
Racing beyond the cosmos on a technicolored rainbow.
His illustrious mane sparkles with rainbow-colored hues in the moonlight,
Shining so colorfully amongst glittering, twinkling stars in outer space.
My Unicorn, white & pure, makes Haste to follow the curving path of a Shimmering Rainbow, with its multicolored arch, back home to my Passionately Devoted Heart.
Using my powerfully gifted imagination,
I can summon my Souljah Starlight,
Awakening Him...
Sending this spirit beast soaring up high throughout the Dynamic Day or Nocturnal Night.....
Higher & Higher...
Past the Orion Constellation and over the Leo Lion Zodiac Star Pattern,
Gliding over a Psychedelic Rainbow,
Striding.....
Hooves Stomping,
Breath Pumping,
Muscles Rippling,
Mane Jumping,
Dancing.....
Making his way like a Phoenix...
Rising up from the dust & ashes of Earth to Higher Heights....
Reaching somewhere over a Bright & Beautiful, Chromatic & Colorful Arch.
Starlight, Starbright...
Is the Reverent & Sacred Spirit Animal Knight
To my Rainbow Bright!

The Sun, Moon & Stars

There is a blinding, beaming, molten orb up past the clouds in outer space.
I enjoy bathing in it's smoldering heat rays.
I am able to feel the sun touch my skin, melting, burning and soaking into my flesh.
It warms, soothes and fires me up to see the sun...
Blazing so Amazing during the day, Showering me with a Dazzling Serenade of Light!

The moon at night shines incredibly bright...
Though it is the lesser light reflecting a sun so luminous & illustrious.
A celestial body so ethereal.....
The moon is my friend.
The man within,
He smiles and frowns at me.

The Stars Twinkle, Glisten and Glitter Up the Night Sky....
Stars constantly flicker, and I wonder why?
So immaculately they are shining millions of miles from earth.
Everyday an angel sends a star to watch over us.
Any star I choose shines its light magically.
Then I know, in my heart of hearts,
I am not, nor will I ever be
Alone.
Because,
God & His Angels, plus Jesus and My Ancestors
Will
Forevermore
Love, Protect and Watch Over Me.

Clouds in the Skies

Clouds are a Marvelous Creation of God!
Floating High Above...
They Wondrously Reveal Secret Symbols & Any Shape the Creator wants to
Give or Make with His Love,
Calling us to adoration using His & Our imaginations...
To witness a Powerful Blessing.
Although Science Says they are simply Cumulous, Stratus or Cirrus Clouds,
God's Wisdom Abounds,
And His creations are Profoundly Inspiring!
When having a cloudy day,
Remember…
After the incredible storm,
Rain Clears Away
Revealing Radiant Rainbows in Grand Display!
If you are lucky, you can spot one, two or three,
Hovering above you Magically in a colorful way.
Their splendor is forever precious to me!
Praise Be to the Creator for letting me see
His Miraculous Glory...
His Awesome Majesty!

Moon

Moon,
My Mighty Moon,
I see you Shining Brilliant & Effortlessly.
Moon,
My Majestic Moon,
You look so Gloriously Captivating to me.
Moon,
My Magnificent Moon,
You Radiate Magical Moonbows Dynamically!
Moon…..
Moon…..
Hovering High up in the Starry Night Sky…
Perfectly.
Moon…..
Moon…..
Your face is Always Smiling.
It tickles me PINK to witness & see.
Moon…..
Moon…..
You are Amazingly Astonishing to me…
A present...
A portrait of God's Lesser Light,
Yet perfectly round when perfectly full,
Glowing & Gleaming Gorgeously Tonight!

Later on,
The moon may disappear,
Covered up & hidden by clouds.
Remember to keep your eyes peeled...
For there are a ribbon of moonbows hovering around the moon in the dark, glittering Night Sky.
A Fantastically Spectacular Array...
Magical Moonbows of Love...

Bravely Arching Around
The Full Moon.
The perfectly centered moon beneath beaming moonbows...
Motivates me in a seductive & provocatively inspiring way.

Today,
On this Wondrous Day,
I Heart You Moon!
Thank you for coming out, so full, to play!
Maker of Dreams Come True.....
For I see Two Moonbows Manifesting.
Let's see if I can spot three...
Glowing & Gleaming
Down upon me.
It would mean so much to me,
If I could make a wish upon your majorly stunning,
Incredibly Heavenly,
Super Superb,
Circular Orb of Miraculously Reflective Light.
A Humongous Star,
Projecting & Radiating
Mighty, Majestic & Magnificent Moonbows
Arching All Around the Moon...
Blazing Bright in the Darkness of Night!

An Early Morning Dream

Today,
I awoke at 3:30am.
I am the Epitome of a Night Owl.
A Lioness, I Growl in my Belly on the Prowl to Break my Fast!
Like a true predator, I hunt down my prey;
I cook up my breakfast Early at Dawn, 4:30.
A Mighty Meal, including Bacon, Beef Sausage, and Portuguese Meat,
Plus Pancakes, Potatoes and Eggs to go on My Plate.
No need to hesitate....
Once I build my appetite at 4:20 with herbal medication wrapped up in a blunt.
Now, we can munch.....
Make no mistake, I can Handle that plate of mine.
I can eat a Horse or a Whole Bovine Cow.
This baby girl needs some more....
Milk!
Ice Cold & Creamy....
2%.
This night owl can now fly away, soaring way up into the sky
Beyond the dark side of the moon.
Soon we will witness the twinkling of Orion's Belt...
Where we'll See & Be Triple Stardom...
As this Ferocious & Fierce Lion Queen stretches her Pure White, Whirring Wings....
As seen in her Dreams.
Miss Night Owl...
This Angelic Being will forever Supremely Reign:
Kind-Hearted, Intelligent, Extraordinary, Superb.....
Giving, Loving and Wise
Yet Never Mean!
Her Destiny is Inspiring....
Like an Early Morning Dream.

CHAPTER 9

My Truth

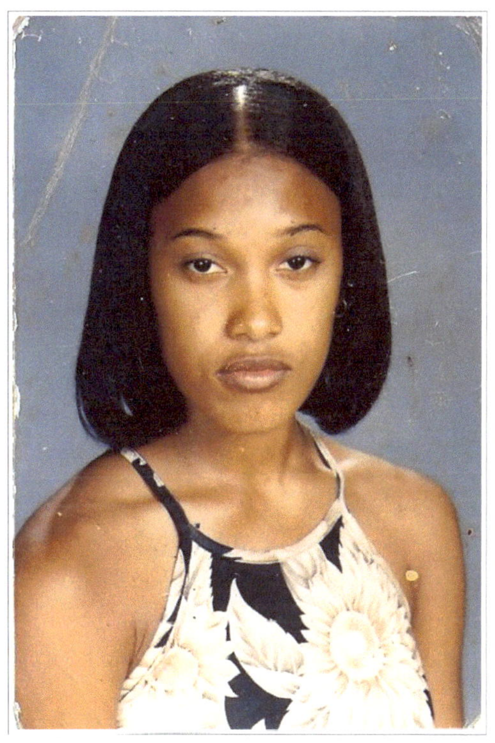

Daybreak Before Nightfall

Light has begun to radiate beneath the horizon.
Daybreak has come.
First, a gentle splash of sunshine...
Lit illumination amidst the dusty dawn with its darkened sky…
Then, amazingly & magically
Pure light filters in throughout the sky, beyond the horizon,
Creeping up slow...
Cascading up all across the early morning, star-filled firmament...
With the Moon still reflecting Sun….
Shining...
Showing Lesser yet just as Brilliant and Vivid next to the Brightest One
Being the Sun…

Sunshine begins to glow, heat up and burn away the dew,
Melting upon and into my supple skin too.
The radiance of daybreak is ethereal:
Glowing, Glorious, Delightful and Magnificently Marvelous in Every Way…
The Sunrise is Serenading my Soul Within…
With Hopes, Dreams, Wishes, and Goals to be accomplished in Every Brand New
Day!

At nightfall, the breath-taking light shall disappear, as the blazing, bright sun descends
Back down below the horizon with an awe-inspiring sunset.

Colors from the omnipotent's paintbrush can sparkle and hover, blended to perfection,
Leaving one dazzled as they gaze amongst the silver lining of clouds.

Red skies at night are a sailor's delight.
Red skies at dawn, and a sailor should be warned.

Other colors abound….
An assortment of hues:

Pink, Purple, Gold, Blue, Orange, Yellow, Turquoise, Serene Green...
With a luminous light surrounding gray & white hovering clouds.

The silver lining is surreal with all the spectacular sky colors created being wonderfully Enchanting.

An inspiration to all those who witness or see...
It is an Artistic Sky Creation that Defies Belief!

Naïveté

My mind is vulnerable, because I am so totally naive.
It is a characteristic trait flaw,
Very Subtle,
Yet it is one that others easily perceive.

Being so fantastically fantasy-orientated, oftentimes I get into serious trouble!
It is only because I am easily swayed and also highly gullible!

I walk a Fine Line on & above Thin Ice!
I always shoot myself in the foot, which is not very kind or nice!

For Myself it is True,
I have the inner third eye as well as the immortal spirit of a child:
Tender, Loving, Special, Kind, Innocent, Heaven-Sent, Humble & Meek.
I aspire to Remain Calm, Positive and Mild...
Never Explosive, Violent or Wild!

It is Extremely Difficult for others to Believe...
There are times when God speaks to me.....
Through His Symbols, His Luminous Signs, His Spiritual Being...
With guidance, love & blessings...
They communicate God's Secrets to me...
Which is Incredibly Hard for Normal People to Fathom or Conceive.

Signs

God is my Savior.
With his eye upon the sparrow,
He watches over me.
I can feel his presence within me, making my heart continue to beat.
Though there are times I hurt so bad that I want to give up and die instead of living,
Thinking I'm better off dead.....
This is when God picks me up again.
Strengthening my soul, God gives me the power and mental control to stick with it.
When I can no longer walk, he carries me through life's obstacles...
Healing my body after suffering through trials I face...
Showing me exactly how great I actually am.
An angelic being sent to earth to help others, shining my bright rays of light.
Many shall take flight to a magically majestic heaven…
With God, Jesus and the Holy Spirit blessing them forever.
Those pure of heart will see GOD.
Call upon him!
He just might respond.
Keep praying...
For you never know what could happen through faith if you simply believe.
Never give up and you will see.
Keep your eyes peeled!
Just call on him and he will be there for thee...
Like he is always there for me.
God is Omnipotent.
I am humble, like a child.
I look up to God and Lord Jesus….
Starry-Eyed.
I can no longer deny…
Genuinely, I love them both until the end of time.
Only they can show me the way…..
By sending me hidden signals & miraculous signs.

Can't Get Right: Due to No Sleep at Night

Some days,
I just Cannot Get Right!
I am too sleepy & groggy,
Too Exhausted,
So Clumsy…
My mind takes Flight!

Dozing off, I try my hardest to stay awake, fighting off dreams.
Wearily I speak, conversing with people who are not there.
But, they exist in my head, all up in my hair.
It is not fair how my powerful imagination mixed with hallucinations can haunt me Daily.

In my walking sleep, I see things like phantoms;
I react & respond, because I feel they are a true reality...
But I am wrong!
These apparitions are Ghostly!

I just want to Get Right....
Yet I cannot, because my eyelids stay closed...
Too taught...
Too tight!

I wonder sometimes,
"Am I dreaming or feigning for rest?"
I will do my best to get to bed Early tonight, because I just Can't Get Right the Next Day if I show no love to my body & brain by resting & rejuvenating in a peaceful way.

Fumbly clumsiness can lead to death!
This result, due to sleepiness, is a mind-numbing pest!
Rest, Rejuvenation and Resuscitation…

Each are a Necessity!
Believe Me,
I should know;
I'm constantly highly fatigued and slow….
Can't Get Right,
I will eventually be paralyzed by exhaustion, glued to tha flo'!

If I stay awake 3 to 5 days without rest,
I will hallucinate.
Let's just go to bed instead…
Get some Sleep!
Close that inner third eye…
It is itching, weeping, still blinking…
Inside my Sleepy, Dreamy Head.

Hit the Ground Runnin'

Everybody get up!
Rise & Shine!
Awaken from your sleepy, DREAMING slumber.
It is time to hit the ground Running!
4am or 4:20 is when God lifts me...
Arousing me somehow...
Enticing me to Rise Up & Come Alive.
I always touch my feet to the ground after I roll out of bed,
Ready to Rumble and go forward Running....
Toke a Blunt or Herbal Cigarette, Walk Tha Dogs and Break the Fast...
Feeding our Stomachs, our HUNGRY Guts!
This ritual comes first, it's a must!

Now, it's time to make moves and speed it up…
Mr. Slothy….
For the longest, most challenging journey begins with the first single step.
Don't forget, we are Spiritual Beings who can accomplish Anything We Put Our Minds
To with Hard Work and Perseverance….
If we have the faith of a mustard seed and unwaveringly believe!
Know, God don't make No Junk!
We are Never No Punks, Never no Lazy Chipmunks!
One must Move It or Lose It!
My Beautiful People...
We will make it, surviving only if we try harder, Becoming Better Everyday,
Forever striving to Rise Up to Higher Heights and Thrive…
Weathering the tempest storms that lie ahead in our lives.
Stay Surprised & Open Minded about life's great encounters.
Be ready, Be prepared…
To take off from the blocks Every morning.
Instead of lying around, sleeping in late like a Sloth,
Hit the Ground Runnin'!
You shall be richer and better off…
In the long run of life!

Making & Riding Waves

Every day,
I want to make some progress,
Whipping up a few Waves....
Stirring things up The Bob Marley Way…
& Style.
I would Love to try something Brand New!
Though I may make many mistakes, falling down….
I can always start Fresh and Anew with a Clean Slate...
Picking myself up off the ground.
I can sing a Happy Song in my Miserable States.
Let us contemplate a Whole New Existence
Together!
No matter what the size of the wave or the weather...
We can hop on, Balancing, and Ride It Out!
If Eddie Aikau Would Go,
I could too, you know!
There is No Doubt that I have what it takes to be
A Great Mother & A Good Wholesome Wife,
Dutifully baking cookies and cakes, cleaning up the place.
Our true home is where I belong.
Let us make WAVES....
Starting over as New People with a Clean Slate!
We can always leave the Mean, Toxic, Sinful Drama Behind,
Climbing Up Out of the Gutter to Live a Better Life!
We are Not Guttersnipes, so start to Act Right!
Respect me and my Beautiful Savant-like Mind…
Riding upon Waves Humongously Large, Super-Sized, Scary and as Huge as the
Bonzai Pipeline…
In Oahu, Hawaii…..
Amazing, Spectacular and Fine…
Like Hawaiian Sophi.

Can We Get Along?
(In Memory of Rodney King)

In the year 2017 of the New Millennium, people are still hateful and mean.
Doesn't everyone still remember a man by the name of Rodney King?
He became a spokesman against police brutality,
Gaining millions of dollars after getting his ass beat.
He coined the phrase, "Can We All Get Along?"
This was back in the 90's
During the riots caused by this man's injustice.....
Heaped upon him because he was black.
People were racist back then, and the police didn't mind a brutal attack
On a poor Black Man.
They used Billy Clubs and Batons to Beat the Hell out of him!
The incident was Vicious & Cruel.

Now,
In this new day and age,
Racism subtly exists.
In modern neighborhoods there is Segregation,
Gentrification,
NRA & KKK,
Even hoity-toity retail establishments that are privately owned,
Turning indigent, poor looking people away...
Even If they have all the money they need to shop & pay.
When will the hateration, racial discrimination, bitterness and spitefulness end?
Ask me again in the next Year of the Rooster, 2029.

In 12 years time...
Let's see if the hues of skin color gradually transform into the browner tone.
We are All mixed up Mulattos...
And I am not alone looking all black and proud...
A beautiful inspiration with lots of melanin and brown pigment.
I am, supposedly, 33% Caucasian and Black 65%.

I used to think I was part Cherokee with Native American blood within me.
Unfortunately,
They say I have only .2% Cherokee.
23andMe explained those, supposed, facts to my racially mixed family.
Maybe, one day, we will all be mixed up looking fine in different hues of brown.
A rainbow of mulattos perfectly pigmented and colorful...
Never feeling down or less than with horrible frowns upon Faces So Sweet...
C'est Magnifique!
It is a shame we human beings could judge so harshly.
Let God judge us; we are the wondrous, miraculous and marvelous creations he made.
We are all meant to be civilized humans beings,
Striving for success & self-actualization,
Never anyone's slave...
Haggards living in shame....
Destitute with Prosperity Up in Flames!
I simply hope and have faith that we will see the light...
Overcoming suffering and injustice...
Living more Righteously!
Loving one another in Peace & Harmony...
Getting Along...
One and All...
Caring for Enemies with Compassion and Love so Pure!
We can stop the violence, ending racism and discrimination....
For Sure...
For Good!
For the betterment of our world,
Our Planet!
We are living in a Hot Melting Pot,
So Stay Calm and Cool Off!
Turn your frown upside down!
Smile through negativity, and try to remain positive with a Positive Perspective and an Optimistic Outlook!
We will survive staying alive, 'cause we care in this brand new day & age.
No need to feel Enraged!
We shall Elevate Our Minds,
Breaking Free of All our Cages!

The Little Bitty Babies

Children are the Precious…
Angelic, Special, Divine & Unique!
The little babies and infants of this world are important & specially capable of
Any Feat.
They each, individually, deserve every ounce of unconditional love:
Courage, Unwavering Support, Attention,
Tender Affection.
They should be constantly encouraged to do their Best.
Their possibilities are Endless,
Because they have Greatness within them which could lead to Great Success.
In this life & the next
They Shall Be Blessed!
God has them as his children, in his loving, devoted hands.
Women be Women…
And Let Man be Man…
Making an effort to Overstand...
All parents of the world,
Must Do Their Job
To the Best of Their Ability.
God will do the rest.
Your Baby Boo is a Bundle of Joy given unto you by God...
A Gift!
It is a Parent's Responsibility to Provide & Strive for Success...
In order to do their Absolute Best for that Little One...
Be it a Beautiful,
Tiny Baby
Daughter or Son.

Transcendence

In order to maintain positivity with an optimistic outlook
So that I may reach
Self-realization & Self-actualization,
I Must Transcend!
I must Transcend Shyness, Failure, Clumsiness, Awkwardness & Despair.
I must Transcend Hate, I Must Transcend Negativity,
I must Transcend Anger, I Must Transcend Confusion,
I must Transcend Fury, I Must Transcend Misconceptions,
I must Transcend Terror, I Must Transcend Destructive Attitudes,
I must Transcend Fear, I Must Transcend Negative Emotions,
I must Transcend Pain, I Must Transcend Hurt Feelings,
I must Transcend Envy, I Must Transcend Paralyzed Feelings,
I must Transcend Sloth, I Must Transcend Laziness,
I must Transcend Anxiety, I Must Transcend Distractions,
I must Transcend Stress, I Must Transcend Abuse,
I must Transcend Nervousness, I Must Transcend Vanity,
I must Transcend Misunderstanding, I Must Transcend Mental Illness
I must Transcend Conflict, I Must Transcend Destructiveness,
I must Transcend Irrationality, I Must Transcend My Ego & My Own Neuroticism,
I must Transcend Disbelief, I Must Transcend Arrogance,
I must Transcend Suffering, I Must Transcend Illusions,
I must Transcend Guilt, I Must Transcend Forcefulness,
I must Transcend Meanness, I Must Transcend Poverty,
I must Transcend Malice, I Must Transcend Temptation,
I must Transcend Misery, I Must Transcend Denial,
I Must Transcend Tribulation, Must Transcend Doubt & Detriment.....

For in all changes of my personal fortune,
Down to the gates of my death,
I Must remain Loyal, Loving and Forever Faithful....
One to Another.
I pray
God grants me the Serenity to attain Transcendence...

So that I may be Fiercely Brave in Peril,
Totally Temperate in Furious Wrath,
Constant in All Tribulation,
Feeling No Crippling Fear…..
For I have the potential for Greatness...
The Ability to Rise, Learning to Endure
In a State of Absolute Bliss
Filled with Harmonious & Peaceful Happiness
Mixed with Perfect Pleasure
Existing on Every Level:
Spiritually, Emotionally, Physically, Mentally, Sexually, and All Internally!

One day,
I will accomplish my life's dreams,
Fulfilling my Destiny...
My True Purpose given to me by God...
Becoming all I Hope, Wish and Pray to Be…
The Ultimate Me…..
Hawaiian Super Sophi!!!

CHAPTER 10

A Rap

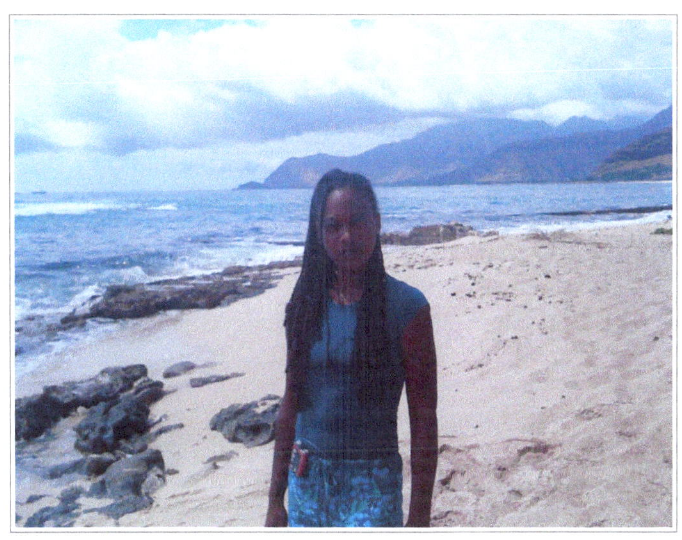

Enraged

I can't be regulated,
I'm way too raw...
My rhymes hit you all up side the brain in yo' head!
I rolled out of my bed & REM sleep to spit this crucial flow...
Some shit that's way too surrealistic and deep!

Busters keep robbin' me on the beat...
Bitch, you can't steal me from me!
Each time, I'm almost forgotten I RISE...
Unscathed, Undefeated, Unparalyzed...
Unshakeable like a Monadnock!

Sorry Sir...
I must look miserably horrible to you right now...
You so scared steady dialing up police.
I'm actually more like a Magical Unicorn...
Not some Hellicorn roaming the earth's streets.

Call me by any name...
I know exactly who I am....
The Greatest, The Dopest, The Flyest of the Fly!
Let my words drip down onto the paper like Real Liquid Gold...
I'm ready to burn a Hole up under all these haters...
And Fly...
Far, Far Away...

'Cause I'm Resilient...
Tough as nails...
You can't do me!
I change, learn & grow from your teachings and life lessons,
Metamorphosizing...
Into something much more....
Much greater than before...

I wish to be!

Feeling All Brand New!
I'm sorry Boo,
I'm not your child or your whore, so don't treat me as such!
I know Much More than you do.....
Sorry Dude,
I don't mean to be Mean or Cruel, but Everybody Wanna Rule The World!

I'm just Makin' My Way Everyday.....
Livin' Life,
No mo' Strife,
'Cause Imma Let It Go....
Movin' on to my next Secret Mission or Scenario....
Stayin' Low.....
Stackin' Dough.....
Overcoming All Odds or any Setbacks that Arise!
Look into my Brilliant Brown Eyes...
I am Alive, Alive, and I will never be compromised...
By any of them Haters!

'Cause I'm a Black Pearl of Wisdom...
Living in a Fucked Up world:
Cold, Dark, Dreary, Sad, Lonely, Greedy, Mad.
I am all alone and on my own.
Only the Stars are my Friends.
It's like Kanye to the West say,
"This is a God Dream!"
It means Absolutely EVERYTHING to Me!

Giving Thanks

I am ever so grateful to be alive.....
Living one day at a time....
I rise to shine...
I am a dime..
Thank you God, for blessing me beyond belief.

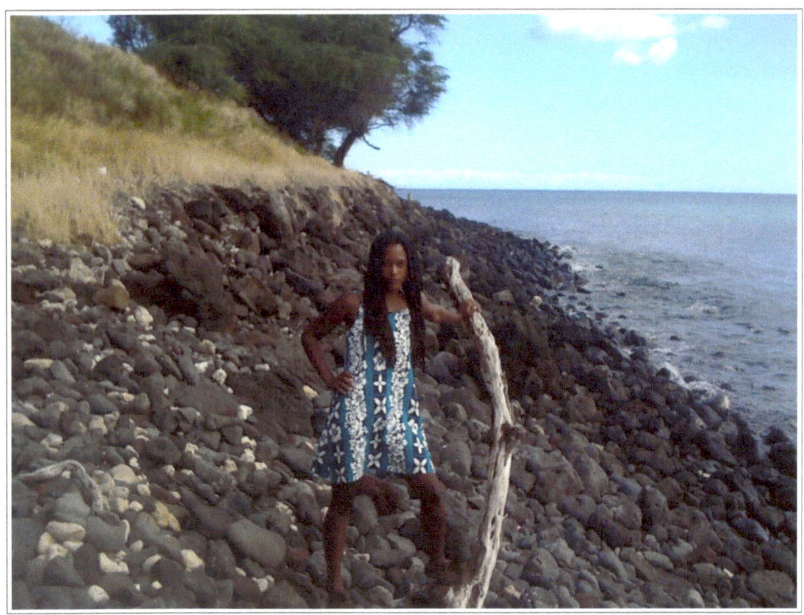

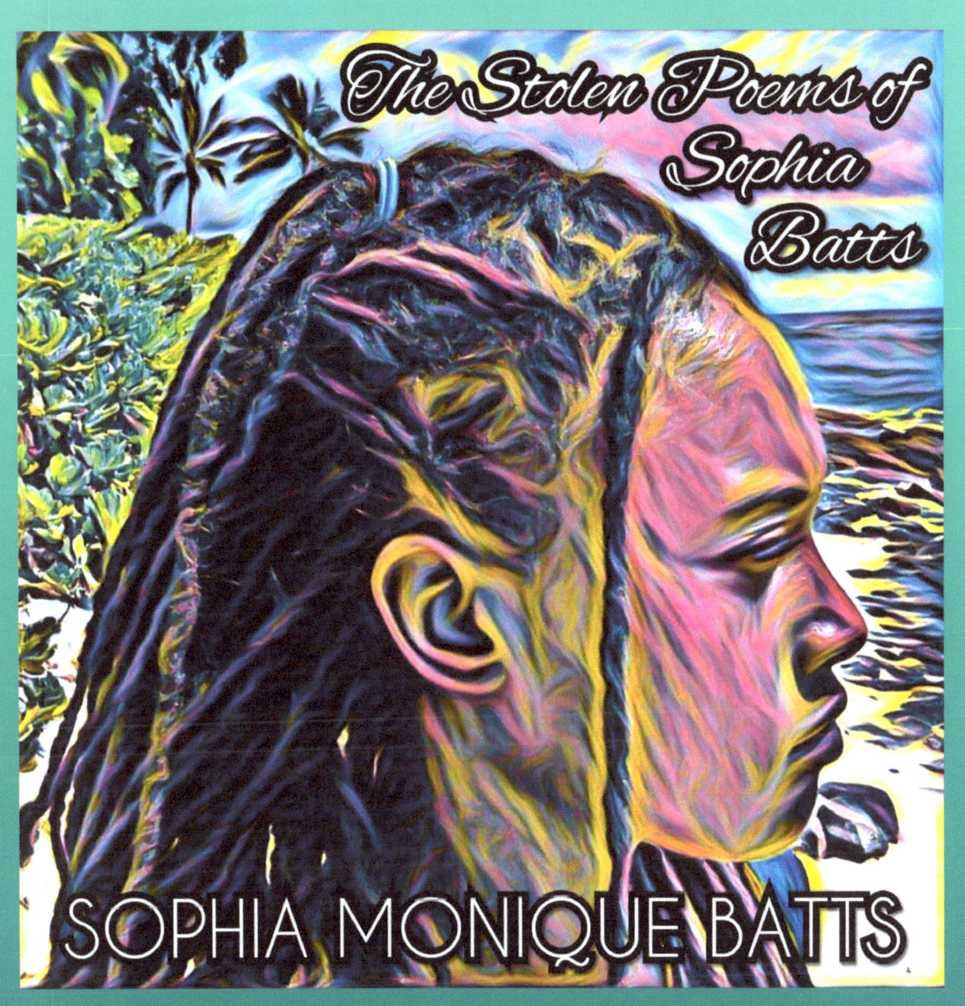
The Stolen Poems of Sophia Batts
SOPHIA MONIQUE BATTS

www.ingramcontent.com/pod-product-compliance
Lightning Source LLC
LaVergne TN
LVHW052254100826
845147LV00001B/43

9780578423722